The San Joaquin,
The Sierra, and
Beyond

The San Joaquin, The Sierra, and Beyond

WILLIAM C. SANFORD

WESTERN TANAGER PRESS
Santa Cruz, California
1994

The author has made every attempt to provide accurate information in this book, but travel, hiking and outdoor sports inevitably involve risks that cannot be foreseen. The varieties of individual human abilities, changing environmental and climatic conditions, and a range of other circumstances cannot be encompassed in any one book. Please let our book help you, but be aware that each individual is personally responsible for his or her own safety.

Cover illustration by Keelin Sabel
Edited by Joanna Gear
Cover design by Lynn Piquett
Text design by TypaGraphix
Maps by Maggie Leighly
Typography by TypaGraphix

ISBN: 0-934136-53-X

Library of Congress Card Catalog Number: 94-60922

Printed in the United States of America

Western Tanager Press
1111-A Pacific Ave.
Santa Cruz, CA 95060

Acknowledgements

A number of people have had key roles in bringing this book to fruition. I want to express my appreciation to them.

- Publisher Hal Morris, President of Western Tanager Press in Santa Cruz.
- William A. Kelly of Scotts Valley, who smoothed out my original manuscript considerably by offering in a gracious manner many valuable suggestions.
- Book editor Joanna Gear of Western Tanager, who shepherded the later phases of manuscript preparation and brought skill, attentiveness and grace to the project.
- Mapmaker Maggie Leighly of Berkeley, typographer Phyllis Wright and cover artist Keelin Sabel, both of Santa Cruz, whose special contributions I value and affirm with appreciation.
- Accuracy checkers. In an early stage of manuscript preparation I had many of the chapters reviewed for accuracy by persons associated with the places described. I am grateful for their willingness to render this service.
- My wife, Jeanne, who has been wonderfully supportive and encouraging of this whole undertaking.

Table of Contents

Introduction   *1*

The Valley

1   Sacramento   *5*

2   Cruising Down the River on a Sunday Morning
      and Afternoon   *15*

3   Riding the Rails at Rio Vista Junction —
      and Elsewhere   *19*

4   Stockton and Vicinity: Highlighting Micke Grove   *25*

5   Modesto/Stanislaus County: Of Almonds, Chocolate
      and a Covered Bridge   *31*

6   Atwater and Merced: Especially Airplanes   *37*

7   San Luis National Wildlife Refuge   *43*

8   Fresno: Love That Zoo and . . .   *47*

9   Selma/Kingsburg: Celebrating the Long Ago and the
      Far Away   *51*

10   Hanford: A Three-Century City   *57*

11   Bakersfield/Kern County: Proud Center of the Southern
      San Joaquin Valley   *63*

Venturing West

12   Shadow Cliffs Lake • Del Valle Lake, Alameda County   *67*

13   San Joaquin Valley National Cemetery   *71*

14   Los Banos Creek   *75*

15   Pinnacles National Monument   *79*

16   From I-5 to I-5 via Highway 25: Beef, Oil, Fruit and Water   *83*

Venturing East to the Foothills

17   Indian Grinding Rocks, Daffodils and Other Delights   *89*

18   California Caverns   *95*

19   Riding Rafts on Rampaging Rivers   *99*

20   Hetch Hetchy   *105*

21   Mariposa: Mining and Minerals   *109*

22   Fun by Some Dam Sites   *115*

Ranging the Sierra Nevada

23   Grover Hot Springs State Park   *119*

24   Triple Play:
    • Columbia Historic State Park
    • A Choice of Caverns
    • Calaveras Big Trees State Park   *123*

25   Highway 108 Country/Summit District of Stanislaus National Forest   *127*

26   A Day in Yosemite Valley   *131*

27   Tenaya Creek and Snow Creek Falls   *137*

28   Taft Point and the Fissures   *139*

29   The Panorama Trail   *143*

30   Tenaya Lake and the Tuolumne Grove   *147*

31   May Lake and Mt. Hoffmann   *151*

32   Indian Ridge and Its Natural Arch   *155*

33   Fresno Dome • Nelder Grove • Corlieu Falls   *159*

34   Sierra Vista Scenic Byway   *163*

35   Huntington Lake and Environs   *167*

36   Kings Canyon   *173*

37   Sequoia National Park   *177*

38   Mineral King   *181*

Beyond the Sierra

39   The Far Side: June Lake, Mono Lake and Bodie   *185*

40   Ancient Bristlecone Pine Forest   *191*

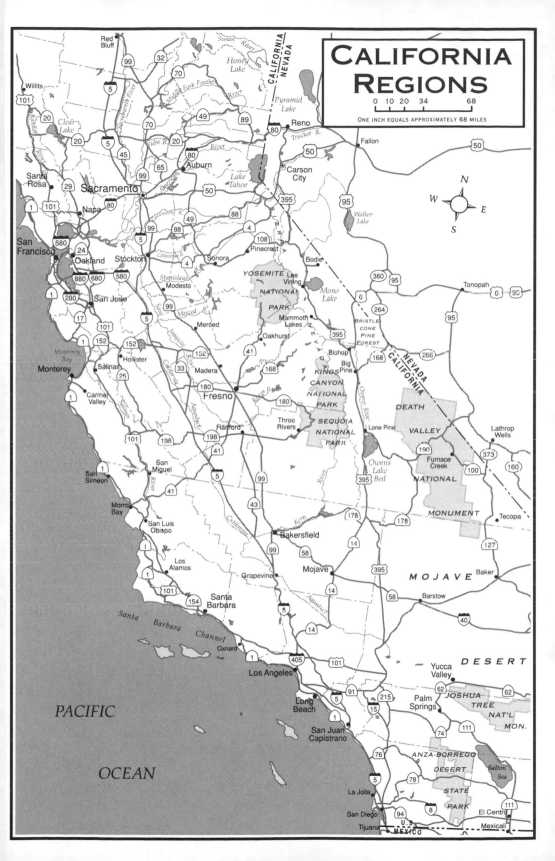

CALIFORNIA REGIONS

0 10 20 34 68

ONE INCH EQUALS APPROXIMATELY 68 MILES

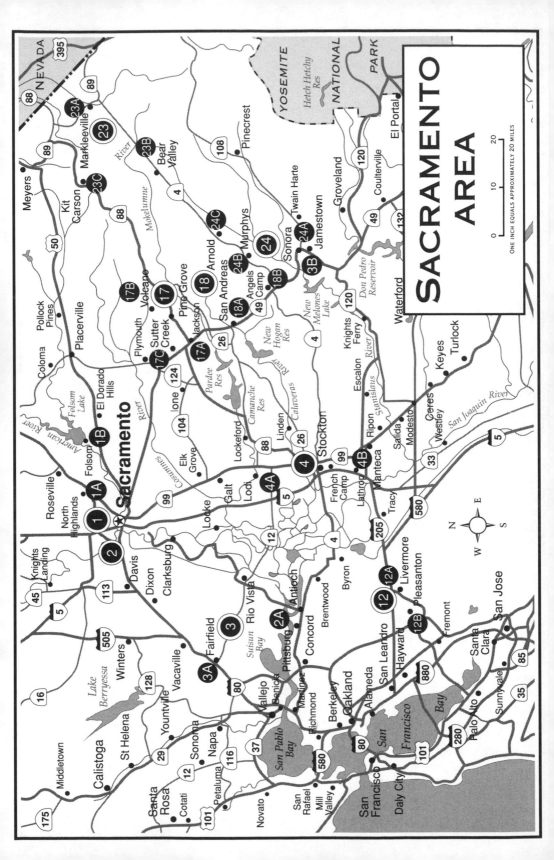

SACRAMENTO AREA

ONE INCH EQUALS APPROXIMATELY 20 MILES

0   10   20

Sacramento Area

1   *Sacramento*
       1A Effie Yeaw Nature Center
       1B Folsom

2   *Sacramento River Cruise*
       2A Pittsburg

3   *Rio Vista Junction*
       3A Fairfield
       3B Jamestown

4   *Stockton*
       4A Micke Grove Park
       4B Oakwood Lake Resort

12   *Shadow Cliffs/Del Valle Lakes*
       12A Livermore
       12B Pleasanton

17   *Indian Grinding Rocks*
       17A Jackson
       17B Daffodil Hill
       17C Sutter Creek

18   *California Caverns*
       18A San Andreas
       18B Angels Camp

23   *Grover Hot Springs*
       23A Markleeville
       23B Lake Alpine
       23C Silver Lake

24   *Columbia Historic Park/Calaveras Big Trees*
       24A Sonora
       24B Murphys
       24C Arnold

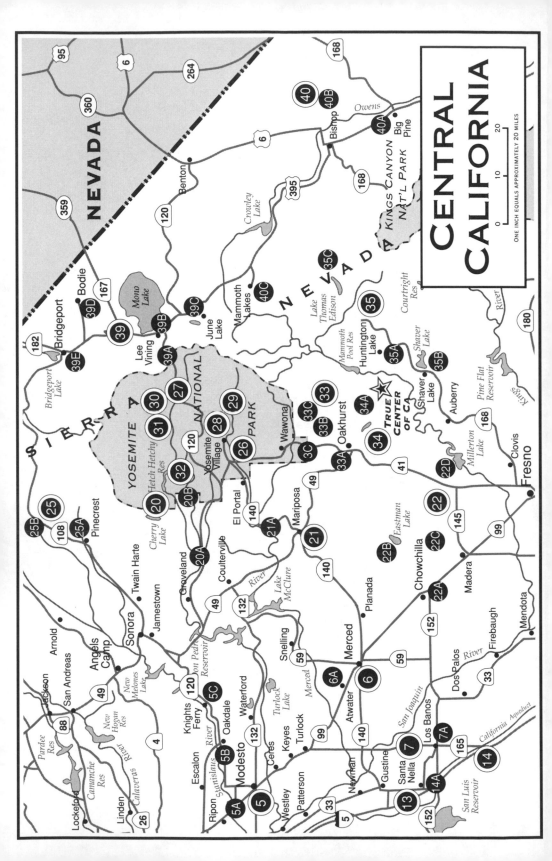

Central California

3 Rio Vista Junction
    3C Yosemite Mtn.–
        Sugar Pine Railroad

5 Modesto/Stanislaus County
    5A Salida
    5B Oakdale
    5C Knights Ferry

6 Atwater/Merced
    6A Atwater

7 San Luis Wildlife Refuge
    7A Los Banos

13 San Joaquin Valley
    National Cemetery

14 Los Banos Creek
    14A Santa Nella

20 Hetch Hetchy
    20A Buck Meadows
    20B Camp Mather

21 Mariposa
    21A Briceburg

22 Dam Sites
    22A Chowchilla
    22B Eastman Lake
    22C Hensley Lake
    22D Millerton Lake

25 Highway 108/Stanislaus Natl. Forest
    25A Pinecrest
    25B Donnell Reservoir

26 through 32:
Pick up Yosemite map at
entrance station for all sites

33 Fresno Dome/Nelder
    Grove/Corlieu Falls
    33A Oakhurst
    33B Sky Ranch Road
    33C Nelder Grove

34 Sierra Vista Scenic Byway
    34A. North Fork

35 Huntington Lake
    35A Big Creek
    35B Shaver Lake
    35C Lake Thomas Edison

39 Mono Lake
    39A Tioga Pass
    39B Lee Vining
    39C June Lake
    39D Bodie
    39E Bridgeport

40 Ancient Bristlecone
    Pine Forest
    40A Big Pine
    40B Schulman Grove
    40C Mammoth Lakes

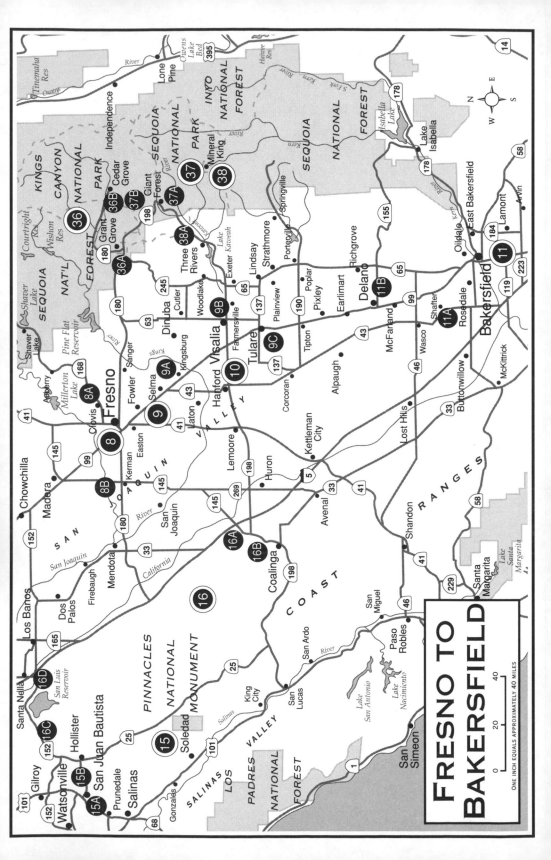

FRESNO TO BAKERSFIELD

ONE INCH EQUALS APPROXIMATELY 40 MILES

Fresno – Bakersfield

8   *Fresno*
     8A   Clovis Lakes
     8B   Kerman

9   *Selma/Kingsburg*
     9A   Selma–Kingsburg
     9B   Visalia
     9C   Tulare

10   *Hanford*

11   *Bakersfield*
     11A   Shafter
     11B   Delano

15   *Pinnacles National Monument*
     15A   Fremont Peak
     15B   San Juan Bautista

16   *I-5 Via Highway 25*
     16A   Harris Ranch
     16B   Coalinga
     16C   Casa de Fruta
     16D   San Luis Reservoir

36   *Kings Canyon National Park*
     36A   General Grant Grove
     36B   Cedar Grove

37   *Sequoia National Park*
     37A   Giant Forest
     37B   Lodgepole

38   *Mineral King National Park*
     38A   Three Rivers

Introduction

I have lived in the great central valley of California most of my life—in Oroville, Stockton, Kingsburg and, since 1980, in Atwater. I'm a valley booster. I admit we sometimes manage a bit of a heat-surplus on certain summer days, and there are some winter days with fog when I'd rather be in Hawaii. Despite those considerations, I like living here, and I love to visit valley destinations as a sightseer. I also like the valley as a launching pad. It's a great starting point for one- and two-day forays into the foothills and the higher mountains beyond. You will see the exciting possibilities as you turn these pages.

True Central California

This book reveals for San Joaquin Valley residents and visitors alike 40 one-day and two-day trips and tells you where to go for some very rewarding experiences. I want your outings to be fun. I don't want you to be cooped up in your car all day pounding pavement over mega-mileages. Therefore, I've settled on a circle of limitation with a radius of 100 miles, a distance which keeps day trips "do-able."

Would you mind spending a moment with your California road map? Put your finger on the spot that you'd guess to be the center of the state. Where did your finger land? On Merced, Madera, Fresno? Actually, you're fairly close; however, authorities place it a bit further east than perhaps you expected. They say that California's center lies on a hillside between the community of North Fork and the San Joaquin River.

I have chosen to cut myself a little slack and make the operative center point for these trips a tad to the north, at the

1

community of Oakhurst, located on Highway 41 between Fresno and Yosemite. Swing a 100-mile radius circle around Oakhurst and you embrace nearly all the destinations detailed in this book (with the exception of a few trips which require going just a little further afield). You include along the Highway 99 north-south axis the territory from the Stockton area right on down through Manteca, Modesto, Turlock, Merced, Madera, Fresno to below Visalia and Tulare. You include also the territory from the east slope of the Diablo Range clear across to the east side of the Sierra.

There you have "true central California" defined: all that part of the state situated within a hundred miles of Oakhurst. And what extraordinary richness and diversity you include! My circle embraces all or most of eleven counties with a total population exceeding two million. I want this book to be a helpful, practical guide for all those residents, and for the many additional folks who will come into the Valley area from further afield.

Trips in Strips

The table of contents will help you picture this book's organization. Think in terms of strips. First we have a strip along Highway 99, down the center of the Valley, Sacramento to Bakersfield. Then we have a strip of trips down the west side of the Valley, along the eastward facing side of the Diablo Range. Next we list trips down the east side of the Valley, generally through the Mother Lode region. Then I trace trips in the Sierra Nevada mountains that entail going to elevations exceeding 4,000 feet. (Let this be a word of caution to folks who experience health problems at high elevations.) Last of all, I write about two trips on the eastern side of the Sierra Nevada range. In every strip the listings run north to south.

The Chapters' Format

I begin each chapter describing a one- or two-day trip.

Next, I suggest **further explorations.** In many cases, there are interesting things to do in a given vicinity that won't fit easily in the day trip as I have outlined it. On the chance that you may want to stay around a second day or return on another occasion, I have listed some other things you can see and do as you follow your own interests and inclinations.

Thirdly, and usually very briefly, I comment on the **best time to go.** Some trips — those in the high Sierra — can only be made (by most of us) when the roads are snow-free. Some trips can be made throughout the year; however, there may still be good reasons for preferring a certain season. You would be ill-advised to take a blossom tour when there are no blossoms.

Next to last I've put some **nuts 'n' bolts.** Here I comment on routes, distances, time allowances — some practical considerations you'll want to review when you're getting ready to actually take the trip.

Finally, there's a sub-heading for **key contacts.** Here you'll find the name and address of one or more places where you can write or call for additional information. The phone numbers may be particularly useful in the event that you want to get up-to-the-minute details on the days and hours a certain place is open and what the admission charges are.

Admission charges are so subject to change and often so variable (a certain amount for adults, another amount for children and seniors, maybe no charge under a certain age) that I've made a conscious decision not to list entrance costs here. By and large, it's wise to have some dollars in your pocket. If knowing exact amounts in advance is important to you, do call ahead. But where there are admission fees, the central California sites mentioned in this guide are generally inexpensive: another good reason to spend some time here.

To Your Enjoyment

Whatever your destination, I think you may expect to relish the 40 favorite outings I've detailed for you here. Climbing Mt. Hoffmann may not be everyone's cup of tea, but, in general, I believe you will have good and memorable days doing any of these trips. You will find yourself commending them to your friends. In many cases, you will want to repeat them. I'm finding happiness simply contemplating all the enjoyment you're going to have as you get out and get going. Have a great time!

Cordially, your guide to true central California,
Bill Sanford

CHAPTER 1

Sacramento

Sacramento is located where the Sacramento and American rivers join. Native Americans resided here for thousands of years before Euro-American activity began in the last few centuries. The Pony Express ended its ten-day dash from St. Joseph, Missouri, in Sacramento, and the first transcontinental railroad started or stopped here, depending upon your point of view. It has grown from a gold rush boomtown to an international center for agricultural marketing. Recently voted among the top ten places to live in the U.S.A., it is capital of the sixth largest economy in the world: California. Still, the more aesthetically inclined prefer to think of it as "Camellia Capital of the World."

So much history! So much happening today! There's no way you can see it all in a day. Still, with a little planning you can sample a lot. You can touch at least lightly on the city's heritage with respect to agriculture, transportation and government. I did precisely this one day in December, and it worked out wonderfully. Given the opportunity, I would happily re-do the whole day with no changes from the way I outline it here.

First stop: Blue Diamond Almond Plaza Visitor Center at 1701 C St. (nearest cross street: 17th). The first tour of the day starts at 10:00 a.m. Plan to arrive five to ten minutes early. Your tour will begin with an excellent 20-minute film, *The Amazing Almond*, that interprets the whole industry from bees fertilizing blossoms to boats ferrying finished products to world markets.

You'll learn that "the almond people" deal in a lot of

superlatives. They have the largest almond marketing organization in the world (about 5,600 growers in the cooperative, which dates from 1910). They operate the world's largest almond processing plant and they ship to some 88 foreign countries. They put their Blue Diamond label on about 2,000 different items, and they will tell you that almonds are California's largest food export.

Following the movie, which is shown in a comfortable theater, a guide will take you to another part of the 88-acre spread. There you'll watch vast quantities of almonds being inspected and packaged. You'll marvel at the sophisticated machines. You may hunger for a taste of the product. Don't worry; management already has plans for you. When you return to the point of beginning, you're offered two choices, and you can choose both. First, you can snack on a free spread of seasoned almonds. I sampled nearly all flavors and couldn't decide which was my favorite, so I postponed my decision-making until a future visit, which I hope will be soon. The second thing you can do there at the retail store is purchase almond products. I urge you to do any buying quickly because you need to hurry on over to . . .

Stop Two: the California State Railroad Museum at 2nd & I Streets. Dating from 1981, the museum has been called the finest interpretive railroad museum in North America. It features 21 beautifully restored locomotives and train cars, and more than three dozen exhibits. Take special note of the "Governor Stanford" and the "C. P. Huntington" and think of how much more comfortable the life of an engineer is today. Strive for a noon arrival and begin your visit with the seven-minute slide show and the 20-minute movie, *Evidence of a Dream.* Both should help to prepare you for what you're soon to see, and to appreciate the sacrifices people made to put rails over the mountains.

Consider this: from the time the Central Pacific broke ground in Sacramento on January 8, 1863, until the golden spike was driven in Utah on May 10, 1869, six years and four months elapsed. The winter of 1866–67 was one of the worst ever. Up to 7,000 Chinese lived in tents even during the winter

snows, and four times entire camps were swept away by avalanches. The average daily progress on Summit Tunnel was
eight inches — and that progress came by working day and night.
A quarter of a mile long, the tunnel took a year to complete.
So, when you look at the mementoes, remember the people:
their energy, their suffering, their true grit!

As for the locomotives, they are innovatively displayed.
You can look down upon one of them with the help of mirrors.
You can look up at another one from a roundhouse pit. You
can walk through the cab of a third with the aid of stairs. I
think the single exhibit I enjoy most when I visit the museum
is the Canadian National Pullman car. It has been wired for
sound and so made to jiggle and vibrate that I feel I'm back
in my youth. I imagine I'm again in a berth while the train
gobbles up track.

The ticket you buy to enter the museum is valid also at
the nearby Central Pacific Station. The self-guided tour takes
you back to the 1870s and requires about 30 minutes. If you
shorten your late lunch break perhaps you can visit it, or you
may have to return another day. You probably need to come
back again anyway, to see the many other historic buildings
in Old Sacramento. Moreover, fully half the populace would
advise you that there's shopping to be done here, too.

Remember, though, that you really can't do shopping today.
You're due at . . .

Stop Three: the State Capitol, facing 10th St. between L
& N. Parking may be your greatest challenge. Once you've
solved that, enter the huge west-facing front doors, bear left,
descend some stairs and seek out Room B-27, the Tour Office.
Try to include in your visit a ten-minute film, *A Legacy Restored,*
shown in a basement room every 15 minutes, while a 27-minute
film, *Too Splendid to Lose,* is screened daily at 11:00 and 1:30.

As for tours at the Capitol, you must make a choice. You
must choose between the Capitol Tour, the Historic Tour, and
the Self-Guided Tour. Both of the guided tours are free and last
about 45 minutes. I opted for the 3:00 p.m. Capitol Tour, which
gave special emphasis to the Assembly and Senate chambers.
As it happened, our guide had only two of us to take in tow.

We enjoyed visiting with her even while marvelling at the beautifully restored building.

Built originally in 1860, the Capitol was found to be structurally unsafe in 1972, and there was talk of tearing it down. However, in 1976 a total reconstruction began, taking until 1982 to complete. The building, restored to its turn-of-the-century decor and splendor, quickly found itself a major sight-seeing attraction. You'll be glad you included it in your day. By the way, your best chances of seeing the legislature in session are on Mondays and Thursdays. On other days committee hearings dominate the legislators' schedules.

Further Explorations

If you're thinking of going beyond the one-day itinerary outlined above, I suggest you write for literature—well in advance of your visit—to the Sacramento Convention & Visitors' Bureau. Read it, hold family council, and choose what seems right for you. Especially valuable is the Visitors' Bureau's *Sacramento Visitors Guide,* which may tell you everything you want to know. It ranges over accommodations, dining and nightlife, sports and recreation, shopping, transportation, and contains a calendar of special events. Besides all that, it's strong on the city's major attractions. I am indebted to it for much of the material that follows.

Sacramento is so richly endowed with rewarding things to see and do that I hope you'll undertake a series of one-day trips, or, if it suits you better, settle in for a several-day stay. You've got a great smorgasbord here. Put on your plate whatever looks good to you. Most of the principal Sacramento attractions can be listed in three clusters. Cluster one will be the highlights of Old Sacramento. Cluster two will be highlights elsewhere in the downtown letter/number grid, all comparatively close together and easily located. Cluster three will identify attractions somewhat further afield.

Cluster One—Old Sacramento

This listing presupposes that you will walk a loop counterclockwise beginning at the . . .

California State Railroad Museum, 125 I St., Sacramento

95814; 916/552-5252, Ext. 7245. Daily 10:00 a.m.–5:00 p.m.; Admission charge. The museum is discussed earlier in this chapter.

Sacramento History Museum, 101 I St., Sacramento 95814; 916/264-7057. Explore the rich romantic history of the Sacramento region. See $1,000,000 in Mother Lode gold, state-of-the-art interactive computer archives and special changing exhibits. Open Wednesday through Sunday, 10:00 a.m.–5:00 p.m. Admission charge.

Central Pacific Passenger Station, Front St. about a block west of the Railroad Museum. The phone number is the same as for the Railroad Museum. The reconstructed station depicts the bustling activities of the 1870s. From the Passenger Depot, train rides are available every weekend from May through Labor Day from 10:00 a.m. to 5:00 p.m. October through April train rides are scheduled on the first weekend of the month from noon to 3:00 p.m. There's a charge for a train ride.

Delta King, 1000 Front St., Sacramento 95814; 916/444-5464. This historic riverboat includes a hotel, meeting facilities, restaurant, theater, shops and a museum.

Old Sacramento Schoolhouse, Front & L Sts., 916/483-8818. Built in the style of one-room schools found in the 1800s, the museum is open Monday through Friday from 9:30 a.m. to 4:00 p.m., Saturdays and Sundays, noon to 4:00, volunteer staff permitting.

California Citizen–Soldier Museum, 1119 Second St., Sacramento 95814; 916/442-2883. The exhibits here reflect California's rich militia and military history from pre-statehood to contemporary times. The museum contains more than 30,000 military papers, documents and memorabilia. It's open Tuesday through Sunday, 10:00 a.m.–5:00 p.m. for an admission charge.

Remember that Old Sacramento offers about 20 dining options and roughly 100 shops.

Cluster Two — Downtown
(an alphabetical listing)

Blue Diamond Growers Visitors Center, 1701 C St. (at 17th), Sacramento, CA 95814; 916/446-8409. Free tours are available Monday through Friday, 10:00 a.m. and 1:00 p.m., by appointment only; call ahead for reservations. The center is described earlier in this chapter.

Crocker Art Museum, 3rd & O Sts., Sacramento 95814; 916/264-5423. Art for all ages can be found in this restored Victorian building filled with early California paintings and sculptures, Asian art, Old Master drawings, contemporary art and photography. Built in 1872, the Crocker is the oldest public art museum in the West. It is open Wednesdays through Sundays, 10:00 a.m.–5:00 p.m. Tours are available. There's an admission charge.

Governor's Mansion, 16th & H Sts., Sacramento 95814; 916/323-3047. The regal 15-room Victorian mansion was home to 13 of California's governors until 1967. Daily tours are offered from 10:00 to 4:00 p.m. on the hour, Thanksgiving, Christmas and New Year's Day excepted. There's an admission charge.

Leland Stanford Mansion, 8th & N Sts.; Sacramento 95814; 916/324-0575. This home of the former California governor, senator and railroad baron, built in 1857, is being restored by the California Department of Parks and Recreation. Phone to inquire about availability of tours. Admission charge.

Sacramento Children's Museum, 1322 O St., Sacramento 95816; 916/447- 8017. Here you find hands-on exhibits and activities for ages 3 to 12 years. The general public is welcome on Tuesdays through Thursdays, 10:00–2:00. Admission charge.

State Capitol, 10th St. & Capitol Mall; State Capitol, Room B-27, Sacramento, CA 95814; 916/324-0333. Open daily 10:00–5:00; closed Thanksgiving, Christmas and New Year's Day.

Ordinarily, the Capitol Tour is offered on the hour from 9:00 a.m. to 4:00 p.m., except that on weekends the first tour starts at 10:00. The Historic Tour usually operates at 10:30, 11:30, 1:30 and 2:30 and features six old offices, including those of the Governor, the State Treasurer and the Secretary of State. The Capitol Park Tour is offered once a day at 10:30, mid-June to Labor Day. You'll see trees from nearly every part of the world and plants from all of California's counties. Whether you take this tour or not, you may well want to seek out the California Vietnam Veterans' Memorial on the east side of the Capitol, nearly down to 15th St.

The State Capitol Museum is open 9:00 a.m. to 5:00 p.m.

daily except New Year's Day, Thanksgiving and Christmas (10:00 a.m. to 5:00 p.m. on weekends in fall and winter). Free tickets at the Tour Office, Room B-27.

State Indian Museum, 26th & K Sts.; Sacramento 95816; 916/324-0971. Display of arts and crafts illustrating the lifestyle of California's earliest inhabitants. Open daily 10:00 a.m.–5:00 p.m. Closed New Year's Day, Thanksgiving and Christmas. Admission charge.

Sutter's Fort, 27th & L Sts.; Sacramento 95816; 916/445-4422. Sacramento's earliest settlement was founded by John Sutter in 1839. Self-guided tours with audio-wands explain the exhibit rooms, which include a cooper and blacksmith's shops, a bakery, prison, dining room and living quarters. Sutter's Fort is open daily 10:00 a.m.–5:00 p.m., except for Thanksgiving, Christmas and New Year's Day. Admission charge.

Towe Ford Museum, 2200 Front St., Sacramento 95818; 916/442-6802. Here you have the world's most complete antique Ford collection featuring 175 cars and trucks. It's open daily from 10:00 a.m. to 6:00 p.m., excepting Thanksgiving, Christmas and New Year's Day. Admission charge.

Wells Fargo History Museum, Wells Fargo Center, 400 Capitol Mall; 916/440-4161. The hundreds of items on display include artifacts, documents, old photos and lithographs which bring to life the commercial history of Sacramento. It's open Monday through Friday, 9:00 a.m.–5:00 p.m., closed on bank holidays. Admission free.

Cluster Three — Beyond Downtown
(an alphabetical listing)

Effie Yeaw Nature Center, 6700 Tarshes, Carmichael 95608; 916/489-4918. The center features live birds and animals in a 4,000 sq. ft. exhibit room, and nature trails through a 77-acre nature sanctuary. Visitors get an up-close look at the plants and animals within the elongated American River Parkway. The Center is open daily except for major holidays. Hours: 10:00 to 5:00. Admission free; $4 parking fee.

Folsom and Historic Sutter Street. The Gold Country begins with the historic city of Folsom, 25 miles east of Sacramento. A state park is within the city on the shores of Lake Natoma.

Museums include the original powerhouse, the Folsom History Museum at the Wells Fargo building and the Ashland Station railroad depot. Nearby Folsom Lake is one of the state's largest reservoirs. The Old Town section of Folsom features 150 shops and more than a score of restaurants.

Nimbus Fish Hatcheries, 2001 Nimbus Rd., Rancho Cordova 95670 (Highway 50 & Hazel Ave.); 916/355-0666. Features King salmon and steelhead trout. Open 7:00 a.m.–3:00 p.m. in summer; 8:00–4:00 in winter. Admission free.

Sacramento Science Center, 3615 Auburn Blvd., Sacramento 95821; 916/277-6180. The facility includes a planetarium, hands-on science exhibitions, an exterior exhibit highlighting native California plants, and a gift shop with science-related merchandise. The center is open Wednesdays through Fridays, noon to 5:00; Saturdays and Sundays, 10:00 to 5:00. Admission charge.

Sacramento Zoo, 3930 W. Land Park Dr., Sacramento 95822; 916/264-5885. Located in William Land Park, this 15-acre zoo exhibits many exotic animals, including 33 endangered species. It's open daily except Christmas from 10:00 to 4:00. Across from the zoo is Fairytale Town, a six-acre children's theme park.

Waterworld USA—Family Waterpark, 1600 Exposition Blvd., Sacramento 95815; 916/924-0555. Waterworld features Breaker Beach, the largest wave pool in northern California, plus 25 other attractions, including the highest water slides in the West. It's open daily 10:30 to 6:00 (closing times vary) from Memorial Day to Labor Day. Admission charge.

Best Time to Go

I would not discourage visiting Sacramento any time of year. However, if you're thinking of making the three stops I described at the beginning of this chapter, I'd make summer my fourth choice of season. That's because summer can be unpleasantly hot and possibly overcrowded with tourists. My first choice? Winter. At all three venues you're protected from the elements.

Nuts 'n' Bolts

Since downtown Sacramento is a straightforward letter/number grid, I don't think there's warrant for my detailing your every driving move. Get a good city map. Identify the three locations you'll be visiting. Move point to point the best you can, being alert to the fact that many downtown streets are one-way. And bear in mind that your minimum time budget is from about 10:00 to 4:00—not counting driving time to or from Sacramento.

Key Contact

Sacramento Convention & Visitors Bureau
1311 I St.
Sacramento, CA 95814-2965
916/442-5542

CHAPTER 2

Cruising Down the River on a Sunday Morning and Afternoon

Once upon a time there was virtually no choice of transportation. If someone wanted to travel between Sacramento and San Francisco, a journey over water was required. There were no highways, no railroads and certainly no airplanes. People traveled by boat. Happily, it's possible to do that still.

Let's assume for the moment that you've paid for your passage and you know the day and hour your boat will depart. Now all you have to do is drive to the Port of Sacramento in West Sacramento, move through the security checkpoint, lock and leave your car in a large free parking area, and board the boat.

Down you'll go on what early Spanish explorers called the *Rio del Sacramento* (River of the Holy Sacrament), often referred to by early-day travel writers as the "Nile of the West." If you are a thrillseeker, the first part this trip may be too tame for your personal taste. In the early going, the sights don't evoke great excitement, but it could well be that something on the quiet side is exactly what you're looking for. Here you can be assured of hours when the phone won't ring. You'll have no concern about highway traffic; deadlines won't loom; the pace of life will slow; stress will fade away. Perhaps you can embrace the whole package as a prescription for lowering your blood pressure.

When your mind isn't occupied with listening to the highly informative commentary over the public address system, you may do a number of things. You can visit with other passengers, read, play cards or dominoes, snack and even dine. It may be enough simply to cast your eyes over the ever-changing outlook.

To be candid, the first 2¼ hours of the trip are only lightly laced with points of interest. Much of that time you are negotiating what amounts to a very large, mostly straight ditch called the Sacramento Deepwater Channel, dredged to a depth of 35 feet.

A made-for-the voyage map is offered for sale on board. Buy one. Not only does it trace in red your route for the day, it shows virtually the whole of the Sacramento/San Joaquin Delta, and on the flip side it has twelve panels of information. While the trip narrator will tell you most of what's in print and a good deal more, it's nice not to need to take notes, and to have something to refresh your memory after the trip. The Delta contains 886 islands of widely varying sizes. There are about 1,000 miles of waterways in the area that are navigable by small boats. Ocean freighters have designated routes to deep water harbors in Stockton and Sacramento. Fifty-six percent of the Delta area is below sea level, while some of the islands are as much as 20-feet below, the earth being kept dry by extensive levees. Farms spread over much of the region, producing important crops such as rice, almonds, sugar beets, tomatoes, asparagus, cotton and safflower.

The first Bay Area town of some size to be seen from your boat is Pittsburg, near the confluence of the San Joaquin and Sacramento Rivers. Nearly half of the full natural runoff of the state's waters is concentrated in this area, and the Montezuma Hills to the north and Mt. Diablo to the south combine to force all this water through a relatively narrow gap.

Mt. Diablo, back of Pittsburg, is a notable eminence. Although its elevation of 3,849 feet isn't particularly lofty by California standards, it has a special claim to fame. You can see more of the earth's surface from Mt. Diablo than you can see from any other peak in the world with the exception of 19,000-foot Kilimanjaro in Africa. How can it be so? There are no intervening mountain ranges to block your view. When the air is truly clear, your eyes can range over parts of 35 counties! Mt. Diablo is one of the most important land survey points in the entire state.

The Delta Travel map/brochure credits Suisun Bay with up to six miles of width and says that the 84,000-acre Suisun Marsh is a "good example of what more than 740,000 acres of the Sacramento-San Joaquin Delta looked like before reclamation and development began over a hundred years ago."

You may find your passage through Carquinez Strait one of the most captivating portions of the cruise. You'll see what still remains of the so-called Mothball Fleet, ships the Navy has in storage in case they are needed in some future time of national emergency. You'll also pass by Crockett, site of the largest sugar refinery in the world, which refines annually almost one million tons of raw cane sugar shipped from Hawaii.

In my opinion, the most exciting section of the trip is from the Richmond–San Rafael Bridge on into the city. The bridge, completed in 1956, is over 21,000 feet long and ranks as the second longest high-level bridge in the world. What ranks first? The nearby San Francisco–Oakland Bay bridge.

In short order, you have views of East Brothers Lighthouse, now a bed and breakfast facility; Red Rock, where Contra Costa, Marin and San Francisco counties converge; Mt. Tamalpais; Angel Island; the Golden Gate; Yerba Buena; Alcatraz Island; and San Francisco. They burst into view almost like the climactic pyrotechnics you see on the Fourth of July, one "wow" sight on the heels of another.

Once in San Francisco, your schedule calls for about two hours of free time for shopping, dining and sightseeing. Adjacent to where your riverboat ties up is the World War II submarine, USS Pampanito. Longer than a football field, it has a distinguished war record. You may want to see its insides. Whether you tour the sub or not, I urge you to walk the short distance to Pier 39, where you can see and hear the sea lions that have been hauling out on the boat slips since January, 1990. One recent census counted 340.

For a general time frame, I'll use the trip I took one Sunday in September. With a ticket from Delta Travel already in hand, I drove to West Sacramento and exited I-80 onto Harbor Blvd., which took me to the Port of Sacramento. Passenger boarding began at 8:30 a.m. and promptly at 9:00 the riverboat pulled away from the dock with almost 400 people aboard. At 4:15—

and after cruising 91 miles—we disembarked at Pier 43½ in San Francisco. Imagine! Over seven hours of being constantly on water in dry California. Remember I still had to get back to my car at the Port of Sacramento. No problem. Chartered buses pulled up right in front of where the riverboat was moored with a choice of departure times: 6:15 , 6:30 and 6:45. I took the 6:15 and I was back at my car about 7:45.

Further Explorations

Some people choose to do this trip as part of a tour group. The day I made the voyage, 77 people had come down from Paradise on chartered buses. You have the option of making the trip from San Francisco to Sacramento on Saturday, but I think downriver is definitely preferable, largely because you save the best for last. You have the further option of spending both Saturday and Sunday making the roundtrip, beginning in San Francisco, but I don't recommend it because of the added cost and the repetitiousness of covering the same terrain twice in two days.

Best Time to Go

For the 1992 season Delta Travel offered twelve Sunday sailing dates, two each month, May through October. It would be nice to avoid an extra hot, extra cold, or extra windy day, but you pretty much need to take "luck of the draw."

Nuts 'n' Bolts

You scarcely need any. When your tickets are mailed to you, you will receive a sheet including a diagram of how to get to the boat and telling you all you need to know about food service on board, how to dress, etc.

Don't forget that you're dealing here with a full day—at least eleven hours, not counting getting to and from the Port of Sacramento.

Key Contact

Delta Travel
P. O. Box 813
West Sacramento, CA 95691
916/372-3690

chapter 3

Riding the Rails at Rio Vista Junction — and Elsewhere

Let's pretend that it's 1940. We recall the opening of the San Francisco-Oakland Bay Bridge to automobile traffic on November 12, 1936, and to train traffic on January 15, 1939. We remember the recent closing of the World's Fair, the Golden Gate International Exposition on Treasure Island, on October 19, 1939. Let's pretend further that at the time we're living in Sacramento. One day the kids say, "Dad, we want to go to San Francisco. We want to visit the zoo. Can we, Daddy, can we, please?"

We might respond: "Okay, let's do it. And we'll take the electric train. We'll go down on the Sacramento Northern."

On the chosen day, off we go on the speedy green cars, all the way to San Francisco. In those days when the electric train reached the Bay Bridge it kept right on going. In those early years of the bridge's life, there were two tracks on the lower deck. Sacramento Northern, Key System and Southern Pacific inter-urban trains all went right across the bay to the city.

Today you can ride over a tiny snippet of that route at Rio Vista Junction, on Highway 12 between Fairfield and Lodi. Making the ride possible are the folks at the **Western Railway Museum,** a project of the Bay Area Electric Railroad Association, Inc. The Association acquired its first streetcar in 1946 and its Museum location in 1960. Today it's an operating railroad — at least on the days it chooses to operate, which are indicated at the end of the chapter.

On the day of my most recent visit three street cars were out and running: a Muni car from San Francisco, a Sacramento Northern trolley from Marysville–Yuba City, and a car all the way from Melbourne, Australia. This last car, bearing the number 648, was built in 1930 and ran up an astonishing 1,292,416 miles before being retired in 1982. It moved a mile and a quarter more while I was aboard!

Besides the ride, I enjoyed my visit to the display barn. There you can pick up a booklet — please return it as you conclude your time at the barn — and read the history of each of the more than two dozen pieces of rolling stock. In the course of your self- guided tour, you can board and walk through a number of these survivors of another time. In the collection are three of four remaining Key System articulated units (two car bodies share a common set of wheels) which plied the Bay Bridge from 1939 to 1958. The cars were built by Bethlehem Steel in Wilmington, Delaware, in 1936. The paired cabins had seating for 124, and often two, three or even four units were coupled together to make a fairly impressive train.

Don't overlook the Museum's book store and gift shop. Its shelves bulge with an array of railroad books, the range of which boggles the mind. Few, if any, stores can match the variety you have here. And there's much, much more: train videos, magazines, tee shirts, caps, pins, postcards, stamps, etc. If you ever need a gift for a railroad fan, here's the place to shop, while you gain the added satisfaction of knowing you're helping to support the Museum.

The Museum grounds include picnic tables distributed among a variety of trees and screened off reasonably well by shrubbery from the worst of the wind that whips frequently through this area.

From time to time the Museum sponsors special excursions, which can include:

• **Twilight Trains.** Dinner at 6:00 and then departure at 7:00 for a 1½-hour ride. Twice in July and twice in August.

• **Ghost Trains.** Two evening departures at Halloween.

• **Santa Claus Specials.** Saturdays and Sundays on the three weekends preceding Christmas. For information and reservations, call 510/778-RAIL.

Though the train is diesel-powered and the speed slow, an excursion will help you gain a sense of valley transportation back in the '20s and '30s. Actually, in those days the Sacramento Northern offered the swiftest transport available between San Francisco and Sacramento, covering the distance in 2 hours and 47 minutes. On some sections of straight track the trains operated up to 75 miles per hour. The Sacramento Northern came into being in 1928 when the Western Pacific bought and merged two predecessor lines: Northern Electric, which ran a line between Chico and Sacramento starting in 1905, and the Oakland, Antioch and Eastern, which had reached Sacramento in 1913. Sacramento Northern also operated street car service in Sacramento, Marysville–Yuba City and Chico. Its inter-city passenger service ceased in 1941.

Further Explorations

Instead of writing a separate chapter, I will link here, on the grounds of similarity of subject, two other railway excursion possibilities further south. One is at Jamestown, a few miles west of Sonora, and the other near the southern entrance to Yosemite National Park.

The State Historic Park at Jamestown is called **Railtown 1897.** Here the focus is not electric, but early steam. Rails all the same!

Daily (10:00 to 4:00) from mid-May through Labor Day and weekends year round, you can treat yourself to a Roundhouse Tour. A piece of Railtown literature describes the experience this way: "The tour begins at the theater in the old freight house. From here you embark on a fifty-minute walking tour into a complex of turn-of- the-century buildings. The six-track Roundhouse, still in use today, contains a variety of steam locomotives, antique passenger cars and the tools and equipment used to maintain them. You visit the blacksmith shop, belt operated machine and carpenter's shops and turntable area. It's all authentic, virtually untouched by time, and is an educational and entertaining experience for the entire family."

But perhaps you yearn to actually ride the rails. To do that you need to choose a weekend, a Saturday or Sunday, from March through November. You can board the *Mother Lode Cannon Ball* and ride for an hour through the Mother Lode foothills.

Departures at 10:30, 12:00, 1:30 and 3:00.

In addition, in the late spring and early fall the *Keystone Special* takes folks on two-hour steam rides, with complimentary snacks on board. These are Saturday evening trips with 5:00 p.m. departures. Through the heart of the summer the *Twilight Limited* goes out for two-hour trips which are embellished with live entertainment and "a Western Bar-B-Que Dinner." Departure: 5:00 p.m.

There are several other special options at Railtown, such as a New Year's Eve Party Train, but for details you'd better solicit exact information from the Park staff. For all special excursions, you should make reservations in advance. Regardless of when you go or exactly what you choose to do, you'll be fraternizing with movie stars—not people you may know by name, but rather engines you may soon come to know by number. Again and again several of the Sierra Railroad's old steamers have been called on to perform both in the movies and on television, especially Number 3, built in 1891. You may have seen it on "Bonanza," "Little House on the Prairie," or "Petticoat Junction."

Railtown, a 26-acre complex, sits astride the Sierra Railroad's main line, which runs some 50 miles from Oakdale up to Sonora and a little beyond. Begun in 1897, the Sierra Railroad is a functioning freight line still, majoring in the movement of lumber. Available on the Railtown grounds are picnic tables and barbecues and the Freight House Gift Shop.

Before leaving the subject of riding the rails, let me alert you to one more possibility. We're still talking steam, but this is steam with a difference. I refer to the ride you can take on the **Yosemite Mountain–Sugar Pine Railroad** behind old Number 15. This is a shay-type engine with its pistons in a vertical alignment, and so geared that, by railroad standards, it can climb steep grades pulling cars loaded with logs. This trip goes through dense second-growth forest over four miles of narrow-gauge track. You'll find it along Highway 41, four miles south of Yosemite, northeast of Oakhurst. Daily steam train operation is generally available throughout the summer and on weekends in the spring and fall. To pin down the details, phone 209/683-7273.

Best Time to Go

With regard to the Western Railway Museum at Rio Vista Junction, I give a slight edge to spring when the grass is green and the valley wildflowers bloom profusely, but really any time of the year can be fine. You do need to attend to the museum schedule: almost always open Saturdays and Sundays 11:00 a.m. to 5:00 p.m. throughout the year. From the 4th of July through Labor Day, the museum is also open Wednesdays, Thursdays and Fridays.

Nuts 'n' Bolts

To drive to the Western Railway Museum at Rio Vista Junction from Stockton (Hammer Lane), take I-5 north 6.9 miles to the intersection of I-5 and Highway 12. Then go west 28.3 miles to the Museum. Folks from Sacramento may wish to come via I-80 and then down Highway 113 through Dixon. At Highway 12, turn right for 4.3 miles. Visitors from the Bay Area should exit I-80 adjacent to Fairfield and continue eastward on Highway 12 to the Museum, a distance of 13.2 miles.

You can have a rewarding, enjoyable visit without spending a lot of time. Very likely one to two hours will be adequate.

Key Contacts

Western Railway Museum
5848 State Highway 12
Suisun City, CA 94585
707/374-2978

Railtown 1897
Sierra Railroad Depot, Fifth Avenue
P.O. Box 1250
Jamestown, CA 95327
209/984-3953

Yosemite Mountain–Sugar Pine Railroad
Fish Camp, CA 93623
209/683-7273

CHAPTER 4

Stockton and Vicinity:
Highlighting Micke Grove

I want to introduce you to an oasis in the Valley. It's a singular place, unusually refreshing. Meet **Micke Grove Park,** a multi-faceted treasure operated by the Department of Parks and Recreation of the County of San Joaquin. This treasure lies only 1.1 miles west of Highway 99 (Use Armstrong Road exit), a mile or so south of Lodi (pop. 52,000); or it can be accessed from I-5. (Take Eight Mile Rd. to Micke Grove Rd.). The original 65 acres of the now 259-acre park were deeded to the county by Lodi area grape grower and philanthropist William George Micke and his wife, Julia, in 1938.

Many things make me enthusiastic about Micke Grove. First, the old-growth valley oaks. What a stately grove of impressive giants! Simply to stroll or sit among them might have the value of a visit to a psychiatrist, if straightforward stress reduction is your need. They impart a sense of peace only a little less effectively than a grove of coastal redwoods.

Another thing I like about Micke Grove is its zoo. Admittedly, it plays in a lesser league than San Diego or San Francisco or Fresno, but it still has much to engage family members of any age. Sea lions cavorting in a fine outdoor pool, monkeys displaying awesome arm strength and amazing agility, and snow leopards, an endangered species, are among the more than 200 animals. There are some absolutely gorgeous birds, too.

Along with picnic tables and a swimming pool, count the amusement area, replete with a variety of rides, another fine feature of the park. Especially so if you have children in your family. Rejoice also in the gardens. You'll find the Japanese Garden near the geographical center of the park. It was designed by Nagao Sakurai, Superintendent of the Imperial Palace Garden in Tokyo for 20 years, and was dedicated by San Joaquin residents of Japanese ancestry on April 10, 1965. On the day of my most recent visit, I found special pleasure in the reflections in the pools. A relatively new building in mid-garden looked like an ideal site for a wedding. The garden keeps its own hours: 9:00 to 1:30 weekends and 9:00 to 2:00 week days. Adjacent is the K. O. Hester Camellia Garden, also dating from 1965. By the way, camellias are named for G. J. Camellus, a Jesuit missionary, who introduced the genus to Europe in the late 17th century.

Just to the east of the Museum — more on that in a moment — you'll find the Sunshine Trail which meanders through a garden of native California plants. It simulates a walk across the state, west to east, in a distance of only 1,250 feet. It's remarkable, I think, that species usually associated with such diverse circumstances dwell here side by side. Consider the range of the regions: from seashore to Coast Range to delta bog to valley to foothills to Sierra crest and on to the high plains desert.

When I drive people into the mountains, I often ask them to point to the spot where we leave the Valley and enter the foothills. It's a tough assignment, but in walking the Sunshine Trail, I picked up a tip: a placard defined the valley floor as having an elevation of from three to 90 feet. All the interpretive signing along the trail is excellent. You'll also like walking across the covered bridge.

Here's one more fine feature: the **San Joaquin County Historical Museum,** open to the public Wednesdays through Sundays from 1:00 to 5:00 p.m. Let me make a confession. On my first two visits to Micke Grove I missed the Museum, once because it was closed, once because I was short on time. I was prepared to believe that perhaps I hadn't really missed a great deal. Wrong! This is an outstanding museum. I would call it "a sleeper." If its budget allowed extensive advertising, I think the visitor numbers would soon skyrocket.

Established in 1966, the Museum has 34,000 square feet of

exhibit and work space. According to a brochure, "The Museum employs a mixture of permanent and rotating exhibits that include local Native American culture, early agriculture, Delta agriculture, transportation, hay and grain, grape-wine industry, tree crops, education, government, early settlement of the county, textile and home life exhibits.

"The Floyd J. Locher Tool Collection is an assembly of over 3,750 different hand-and-foot powered tools representing 19 trades that have been practiced in San Joaquin County and California. The tools date from the late 16th century through the mid-20th century. The collection is the most complete west of the Mississippi River and is of national signficance."

The intriguing displays are distributed among at least seven separate buildings where there's something for almost any interest. Here's a great collection of harnesses and saddles; there's a one-room school house, vintage 1870; here's a kitchen ready for a session of canning 1920s style; there's a photo of the old riverboat "T. C. Walker" that used to take passengers from Stockton to San Francisco overnight. If old tractors appeal to you, you should be as happy as a bear just handed a honeycomb. There are displays of quilting, weaving, basket making . . . axes, planes, saws, mallets, levels. If some family member should tire here at the Museum, send 'em over to the zoo.

Add it all together and arrive at this conclusion: sometime you must quit your headlong dash up and down Highway 99 or I-5 and turn aside to enjoy this welcoming oasis in our great Central Valley.

Speaking of dashing up and down Highway 99, let me fit in here a little something about a significant feature of the highway. I'm thinking of oleanders. The information I want to share about them comes from the March/April 1992 issue of *Motorland.* There, in a short article, Leo Levenson tells much that I found of great interest.

The oleander plant—though it hails from Europe and Asia—acts as if it were expressly engineered for the dire circumstances it routinely endures along California's freeways. It can withstand considerable drought and freezing. Once established, it requires no watering, no fertilizing, no pesticides.

Auto exhaust fumes, wind-whipping, and even too close encounters with stray vehicles don't destroy its composure. It endures, prevails and even thrives! The first plantings in freeway median strips were done in the Sacramento area in the 1940s. The idea initially was to reduce glare from oncoming headlights, and the beautiful red and white and pink flowers came along as a happy bonus. Even its poisonous nature has a plus side: deer won't eat it.

So, as you make your way to Micke Grove, hold a thankful thought for the oleanders. As for the Grove itself, allocate several hours and some money, because admission is charged first to the park, and then again for the zoo.

Further Explorations

If you're in the area and really want a second and totally separate place to visit, I'd recommend a stop at the lovely 200-acre campus of the **University of the Pacific** at 3601 Pacific Ave., Stockton 95211. It is located along the Calaveras River (itself not much to look at) and contains 90 buildings plus athletic facilities. Students trained to offer visitors interesting tours will show you around. Tours leaving from the Admissions Office located in Knoles Hall are usually available Monday through Friday, at 11:00 and 2:00; and tours depart from Burns Tower on Saturdays and Sundays at 1:30. You're encouraged to call a day or two ahead (209/946-2211) so that guide service can be planned to match visitor requirements. Parking tip: an area is reserved for visitors just inside the campus at the intersection of Pacific Avenue and Stadium Drive.

Pacific's roots extend to 1851 when Methodist missionaries formed California's first chartered university in San Jose. The school relocated to Stockton in 1924. Today the Stockton campus embraces a coeducational student body of approximately 3,800 students. Besides the liberal arts college, there are a number of professional schools: Business and Public Administration, Education, Engineering, Pharmacy and the Conservatory of Music. Additionally, Pacific has under its wing a School of Dentistry in San Francisco and McGeorge School of Law in Sacramento.

Three more Stockton area attractions deserving of your consideration:

• **Clever Planetarium,** at Delta College, 5151 Pacific Ave.; 209/474-5110. Here you'll find weekend star shows that describe seasonal stars and astronomical events. When? On Friday and Saturday nights at 7:00 and on Sunday afternoons at 2:00. (But not necessarily every weekend. Phone to confirm show dates). On week days school field trips can be arranged. Phone 474-5112 to make arrangements. Admission charge.

• **Haggin Museum,** Pershing Ave. at Rose St.; 209/462-4116. The Museum's historical exhibits relate primarily to the history of Stockton and San Joaquin County. Exhibits focus on Captain Charles M. Weber, Stockton's founder. The art collection is comprised mostly of 19th century French and American paintings. Free admission.

• **Oakwood Lake Resort,** 874 E. Woodward Ave., (a few miles southwest of) Manteca, 95336; 209/239-2500. Oakwood Lake Resort is a 300-acre park with a 75- acre stocked lake. The park's best known attractions are the water rides. They include nine waterslides, a Rapids Ride, Turbo Tube, and Kiddie Slide. There's a 17,000 sq. ft. pool designed for the family, picnic facilities and more. You can even stay over in one of 360 RV sites, or in an area dedicated to tent camping. Admission charge. Full Day and Half Day tickets available.

A note about the host city: Stockton was originally established in 1849 by a German immigrant named Charles M. Weber (1814-1881). Weber came to the U.S. in 1836 and to California in 1841. He secured a land grant from Mexican Governor Manuel Micheltorena at a most propitious time: just when thousands were rushing to the Mother Lode in quest of gold. Stockton was a key supply point, connected as it was to virtually the whole navigable world by the San Joaquin River. The city was incorporated on July 23, 1850 — more than a month before California officially achieved statehood. Authentically recreated rooms from C.M. Weber's home are among the fascinating displays at the Museum out in Micke Grove.

Best Time to Go

Thinking of Micke Grove in particular, it depends somewhat on what you want to do. If you're not intent on swimming, then I'd recommend spring or fall. Both seasons offer some ideal days, temperature exactly as you like it.

Nuts 'n' Bolts

If you're coming north on Highway 99, use the junction with Highway 88 as a reference point. It's 7.2 miles from there to the Armstrong Road exit. If you're headed south on 99 from Lodi, figure only 2 miles to the Armstrong Road exit.

It's hard to say how much time you should budget. It may not be worth paying your way in unless you have an hour or two, but you could stay much longer than that and not run short of things to see or do.

Key Contacts

San Joaquin County Parks and Recreation
4520 W. Eight Mile Rd.
Stockton, CA 95209
209/953-8800 or 331-7400

San Joaquin County Historical Museum
P. O. Box 21
Lodi, CA 95241
209/368-9154 or
from Stockton 463-4119.

Stockton/San Joaquin Convention & Visitors Bureau
46 W. Fremont St.
Stockton, CA 95202
209/943-1987

CHAPTER 5

Modesto/Stanislaus County:
Of Almonds, Chocolate,
and a Covered Bridge

Now we're in Stanislaus County, which has the thriving city of Modesto (1990 population 165,000) as its county seat. We begin our excursion in a small community called Salida, on Highway 99 about 2½ miles north of Modesto's Standiford Road. It's important to consider the question of *when* near the start. Why? Because two-thirds of what you want to see on this trip can't be seen on weekends. So if you don't have a week day (non-holiday) available, put this whole chapter on a back burner.

We begin with almonds. When you enter the **Blue Diamond Growers Store**—open any weekday 10:00–5:00—you may notice a wall poster almost running over on the subject of almond-ology: "California produces enough almonds to fill the world's largest ocean-going bulk carrier almost ten times. ... There are five main varieties grown in California: Nonpareil, Mission, California Blend, Neplus and Peerless. ... California harvests 61 percent of the average world crop, Spain 17 percent, Italy 8 percent. California has enough acres planted in almonds to cover more than half of the state of Rhode Island including its bays and rivers. ... California grows enough almonds to provide every man, woman and child in the United States with 850 kernels each year."

If you want to learn more than that, visit the room that shows the 22-minute film that tells the whole almond story from orchard to world-wide distribution. This is the same film you

31

can see at the Blue Diamond facility in Sacramento. (See Chapter 1.) Also as in Sacramento, you can snack here. Almonds flavored a dozen different ways are available in as many pitchers and you can pour the taste treats into your hand and call it brunch. Consider taking some home for family and friends.

Now I'm suggesting that you chase your almonds with chocolate. For your second stop, simply drive east about 16 miles to Oakdale and specifically to the **Hershey's Visitors Center** near the center of town.

The Oakdale Hershey's plant dates from 1965 and employs 500 to 700 people in three shifts. It ships all over the American West and to countries throughout the Pacific Rim, although its output is supplemented by three other Hershey plants located in Hershey, Pennsylvania; Stuarts Draft, Virginia; and Smith Falls, Ontario, Canada.

Here your opportunity for a plant tour is limited to weekdays from 8:30 to 3:00. It used to be that visitors drove directly to the plant; however, in 1990 the downtown visitors center/company store was built, and now visitors assemble themselves there. They are then transported about a mile and a quarter to the plant by shuttle bus for a half hour tour.

When the visitors are really flowing, as they are in summer to the tune of about 1,200 per day, your wait for a tour may be very brief. In slower times, it may be as long as half an hour, but during such a wait you can watch an interpretive video, and you can spend money on a wide range of souvenirs and snacks ranging from cookies to Kisses. Speaking of Kisses, take special note of the tops of the light poles outside the plant: Hershey Kisses beyond all doubt. However, more enticing to the palate are those you'll see being made inside.

You'll see a vast bay of conching machines which agitate huge tubs of hot chocolate for 72 hours continuously, and you'll see a range of chocolate bars and Reese's Peanut Butter Cups streaming off the various production lines. Fascinating and mouth watering, it's altogether a great tour — at the end of which a complimentary chocolate bar awaits you!

Incidentally, Hershey's Visitors Center hours differ from the tour hours in two ways. The Center remains open daily until 5:00 p.m. And it is also open Saturdays from 10:00 to 4:30, but there are *no tours* on weekends.

Ready for the third attraction? Drive east another 12½ miles to the hamlet of **Knights Ferry** on the Stanislaus River. Knights Ferry was named for a gold rush entrepreneur named William Knight, who also lent his name to Knights Landing in Yolo County, north of Sacramento. Knight was killed here in a gun fight in 1849, his quick temper triggering his untimely demise.

The magnet for many in this area is the **covered bridge,** at 300 feet the longest west of the Mississippi. It was built in 1864, replacing a bridge washed away in the winter of 1862. Closed to car traffic, it welcomes your footsteps and certainly calls for you to exercise your camera. If you like to collect auditory memories, you might like to record the sound your footsteps make as they take you over the old wood flooring.

Don't limit your attention to the bridge. Near it the U.S. Army Corps of Engineers — which is in the recreation business far in excess of your expectations — has a fine Information Center open weekdays 8:00 to 4:00 and weekends 10:00 to 4:00 from Memorial Day through Labor Day. Spend awhile inside. It offers a number of pertinent video tapes which you can view on request and a room which is a sort of mini-museum. Exhibits treat local history, area Native Americans, current recreational options, and more. One cluster of three panels identifies a total of 27 native animals, birds, and plants, while taxidermy allows up-close inspection of a beaver, bobcat, raccoon and golden eagle.

A few paces up-river you can inspect what remains of a hydro-electric plant that began producing power in 1899. Observe, too, the old mill office and residence built of stone probably in the year 1854. On the south side of the river you'll find picnic tables and restrooms.

Further Explorations

A pamphlet produced by the Oakdale Visitors Bureau (590 N. Yosemite Ave., Oakdale, CA 95361), which you can pick up at the Hershey's Visitors Center, brings to your awareness a range of other area options. The Corps of Engineers has a number of recreation-oriented properties along the **Stanislaus River** over a span of 59 miles. The river lends itself to kayaking, canoeing, fishing, and swimming. Park hours are 6:00 a.m. to dusk. If whitewater rafting lures you, the Stanislaus offers stretches suitable for all levels of skill and experience, from really slow going for the novice to turbulent chutes which will challenge—and threaten—the old pro.

Now before I direct your attention further south in the San Joaquin Valley, let me list for you quite a variety of additional things you may wish to explore in Stanislaus County and in the Greater Modesto Area.

• **Bloomingcamp Apple Ranch,** 10528 Highway 120, Oakdale; 209/847-1412. See how homemade cider is processed. Cider, apples, nuts, and pies are available. Also a gift shop, picnic area and duck pond. Hours: 9:30 a.m.–5:30 p.m. Open daily from July to Thanksgiving and Wednesday through Sunday from Thanksgiving to July.

• **Central California Art League Gallery,** 1402 I St., Modesto; 209/529-3369. The gallery exhibits paintings, sculpture, graphics and selected crafts. Hours: Monday–Saturday from 10:00 a.m. to 4:00 p.m. Groups should phone ahead for a docent escort. Free admission.

• **Great Valley Museum of Natural History,** 1100 Stoddard Ave., Modesto, 209/575-6196. This museum offers exhibits of natural habitats of plants, animals and complete ecosystems found in the Central Valley. Hours: Tuesdays–Fridays, noon–4:30 p.m., Saturdays, 10:00 a.m.–4:00 p.m. Closed Sundays and Mondays and during August. Free admission.

• **Hilmar Cheese Company,** 9001 N. Lander Ave., Hilmar, 209/667-6076. Here visitors can watch cheese production through viewing windows. They can also taste cheese and make purchases from the gift shop. Hours: Monday–Saturday 9:00 a.m.–5:30 p.m. If you would like a plant tour and can organize a group of ten or more people, call the company a few days before you want the tour, and a guide will be enlisted for the occasion. Phone: 209/667-6076.

• **McHenry Mansion,** 906 15th St. (corner of 15th & I Sts.), Modesto, 209/577-5341. This Victorian–Italianate mansion was constructed in 1883 by one of Modesto's first families. Hours: Tuesday–Thursday and Sunday, 1:00–4:00 p.m. Group tours available by calling 577-5344. Free admission.

• **McHenry Museum,** 1402 I St., Modesto, 209/577-5366. Displays of early Modesto and Stanislaus County history. Hours: Tuesdays–Sundays, noon–4:00 p.m. Group tours available. Free admission.

• **Miller's California Ranch,** 9425 Yosemite Blvd/Hwy. 132, Modesto, 209/522-1781. Collection of rare vehicles dating from 1885 and an old-fashioned general store. Tours by appointment only.

• **Modesto A's** (professional baseball team), John Thurman Field, 501 Neece Dr., Modesto, 209/529-7368. Minor league affiliate of the Oakland A's. Season runs from April–September.

• **Water Slides**

— **Big Bear Park,** Waterford, 209/874-1984. Picnic areas, swimming, water slide, miniature train ride, clubhouse, campground and 120 RV hookups.

— **Bogetti's Orchard,** Vernalis, 209/523-2642 or 835-8972. Picnic area, swimming, water slides, RV park and restaurant.

Best Time to Go

Most things on the menu above you can do any time of year. However, if water sports figure in your plans, then of course you must target summer.

Nuts 'n' Bolts

To begin the suggested itinerary, leave Highway 99 at the Salida exit. Go east on Highway 219 (Kiernan) two-tenths of a mile and then turn right on Sisk Road for three-tenths of a mile. There you are at the Blue Diamond Growers Store.

Leaving the store, go back out to Highway 219, turn right and proceed 5 miles to where Highway 219 ends at McHenry (Highway 108). Turn left here on Highway 108 and follow the signing for Riverbank (First St. in 4.9 miles) and Oakdale, an additional 5.8 miles (to S. Yosemite Ave. = J-14). Turn right one block and left ½ block. There you are at Hershey's.

Leaving Hershey's, return to Highway 108 (120 has just blended in to share the route for awhile), turn right and drive eastward (toward Sonora) 11.4 miles. Note the sign indicating a left turn toward Knights Ferry. Now an additional 1.2 miles will bring you across the Stanislaus River bridge to a stop sign. Turn right and immediately right again and ease into the parking area adjacent to the Corps of Engineers Information Center.

If time constraints are not severe, you might like to return most of the way to Oakdale on the north side of the river (rejoining Highway 108/120 from Orange Blossom Road).

What I have described above can be crowded into a half day (roughly 4 hours).

Key Contacts

Modesto Convention & Visitors Bureau
1114 J St.
P. O. Box 844
Modesto, CA 95353
209/577-5757; Events hotline: 577-3848

Blue Diamond Growers Store
4800 Sisk Rd., (Salida)
Modesto, CA 95356
209/545-3222.

Hershey's Visitors Center
120 S. Sierra St.,
Oakdale, CA 95361
209/848-8126

U.S. Army Corps of Engineers
18020 Sonora Rd.
P. O. Box 1229
Knights Ferry, CA 95361
209/881-3517

CHAPTER 6

Atwater and Merced: Especially Airplanes

Bordering Castle Air Force Base, which is due to close in 1995, is an exhibit many residents of the area hope will never close: the **Castle Air Museum.** Before I comment on the Museum, I want to orient you geographically. Atwater and Merced both lie along Highway 99, roughly halfway between Stockton and Fresno. Today they are reaching out to touch each other. The Air Museum is best accessed just south of Atwater via the Buhach Road exit from Highway 99.

This Museum, which currently attracts over 125,000 visitors a year, has both indoor and outdoor exhibits. As you approach the Museum site, it's the outdoors that captures your attention: more than 40 military aircraft! Most are American, and they represent fully a half century of military aviation history.

Much of that history comes alive if you join a tour conducted by one of the volunteer guides. I had the good fortune to have as my tour conductor retired pilot Harry Darlington, who has flown ten of the different models of planes in the exhibit. And what a treasure trove of information and personal experiences he is! As our party stood before a World War II B-17, Harry had these statistics on the tip of his tongue: 12,800 were built; 8,000 were lost; each carried a crew of ten. He led us to a early model B-52. "With aerial re-fueling, it could go anywhere in the world—and return," he said. "It carried a crew of six. It could be loaded with up to 108 500-pound bombs." That's 54,000 pounds or 27 tons!

Cargo planes and fighters contribute significantly to the

display, as do a couple of planes from other countries, notably Britain's Vulcan bomber, last used offensively in the Falkland Islands War of April–May, 1982. For my wife and me, the star of the show was the spy plane, the SR-71 Blackbird. Some of what Harry told us about it skirted close to being beyond belief. He said it could climb to 80,000 feet and fly at a speed of 2,400 miles per hour. A Blackbird once flew from Los Angeles to Washington, DC, in an hour and four minutes. A shot fired from behind it can't catch up, so it's faster than a speeding bullet; and it's virtually invisible to radar. This triumph of aeronautical engineering is all by itself reason enough for a stop!

For a half century the mission of Castle AFB has been the training of crews for B-52 bombers and KC-135 tankers.

I mentioned indoor exhibits. Static displays, a snack bar and a gift shop could lure you indoors. You'll find the latter two in the building adjacent to the parking lot, while the displays are in a second building in back.

Now while you're in Atwater anyway, I want to encourage you to stop at the **Bloss Home** and garden on Cedar Avenue between First and Second Streets. The Bloss Home was the residence of Atwater's first mayor, George S. Bloss, Jr. (1874–1963). He led the city twice, from 1922 to 1928, then from 1942 to 1948. Tours of the home are offered only on the third Sunday of each month between 1:00 and 4:00 p.m. That's pretty limited, but if the camellias and/or the roses are in bloom, they warrant a stroll through the garden.

Something else in the garden commands attention: a couple of redbuds. I can imagine your thinking: "So what? I can see redbuds by the hundreds along the highway into Yosemite and many other places." That's true. However, I'm going to claim that the two redbuds in the Bloss Gardens are the biggest in the world. I have always considered redbuds a bush or shrub; these are trees pure and simple. I measured their circumference one evening, and it was tough because I had no assistant with me. But I persevered and left persuaded that the larger one, three feet above ground level, has a circumference of ten feet six inches, and the other one a circumference of seven feet nine inches. Go ahead, tell me where you've seen redbuds larger than those. I measured a huge deodar cedar close by for comparison, and it had a circumference of eight feet ten inches.

I must alert you to something else about the home or risk damaging my reputation as a rail fan. Upstairs there's a model railroad extraordinaire. It's a representation of the Yosemite Valley Railroad which operated from 1907 to 1945 and covered the 77 miles from Merced to El Portal. It is usually open to the public the same hours as the Bloss Home (3rd Sunday of every month, 1:00–4:00.)

Do you yearn for something more in your day? If so, I suggest you drive on into Merced (about seven miles) to the old **Merced County Courthouse.** It was dedicated on May 7, 1875. The architect was Albert A. Bennett, who also had a hand in the design of the Capitol in Sacramento and a number of other county courthouses. Extensively refurbished in 1982, the old courthouse has won a listing on the National Register of Historic Places.

From time to time it presents special exhibitions. On the day of my most recent visit, three rooms were devoted to a display of nearly two dozen wedding dresses dating all the way from 1870 to 1989. One room showed the county treasurer's office as it appeared in the 1920s. In addition, there were artifacts from a Taoist Temple, a blacksmith shop, and a school room of the early 1900s. Eye-catching was a human-drawn fire engine built in Pawtucket, Rhode Island, in 1853. Most visitors find the beautifully restored Superior Court Room of special interest. It served the county for 76 years (1875 to 1951). The Courthouse Museum is open to the public Wednesdays through Sundays from 1:00 to 4:00 p.m. No admission charge, but donations are encouraged.

Further Explorations

If you have children, a stroll through the small **Applegate Zoo** in Merced might be a nice add-on to your day. It is easily found at the intersection of ''R'' St. and West 25th St. Hours: 10:00 to 5:00.

Are agricultural implements a special interest? If so, consider a visit to the Merced area's most recent tourist attraction, the **Agricultural Museum of Merced County,** which opened officially Nov. 25, 1992. It occupies a three-acre site just east of the city of Merced on Highway 140 East, the road to Yosemite.

A lot of what's on display resides in a new 150-by-40-foot steel building which is about the only new thing around. Nearly everything else goes a long way back. There's a coffee grinder that dates from 1885, tractors built as early as 1905, a World War I era gas station, and a surprising variety of gas engines which still run today. From the old household appliances, including washing machines, you can get a feel for how life was lived in this vicinity in the 20s and 30s.

Some of the larger items are displayed outdoors, and they have attracted sightseers from as far away as Germany and Japan. Credit owner Charlie Parish and collector Johnny Ramondini with bringing this historically important museum to birth.

The Merced and Atwater Chambers of Commerce have literature containing a few other thoughts. If you contact one of the Chambers, ask what progress the California Firefighter's Historical Society has made on its proposed **Fire Museum.** Important details were not yet fixed when this book was being prepared for publication, but I believe this will be a sight worth seeing.

Best Time to Go

I would avoid the hottest, the coldest, the wettest and windiest of days, but there's no season of the year that I would rule out categorically. As far as the Bloss gardens are concerned, March is probably prime time.

Keep in mind the Castle Air Museum hours: 10:00 to 4:00 daily, except Thanksgiving, Christmas, New Year's Day and Easter. Free tours are offered at 10:30 and 1:30. Group tours (for 10 or more) can be scheduled by special arrangement.

Nuts 'n' Bolts

Are you coming to Atwater from Fresno? from Stockton? In either case, budget about an hour and a quarter of driving time. Once on Highway 99 near Atwater, look for the Buhach Road exit. Drive north about two miles to Sante Fe Dr. and turn left immediately after crossing the railroad tracks. Castle Air Museum will be on your right in 200 yards.

Key Contacts

Atwater Chamber of Commerce
1181 3rd St.
Atwater, CA 95301
209/358-4251

Merced Chamber of Commerce
1880 N St.
Merced, CA 95340
209/384-3333

Castle Air Museum
P.O. Box 488
Atwater, CA 95301
209/723-2178   Call to confirm tour availability

Merced County Courthouse Museum
21st and N Sts.
Merced, CA 95340
209/385-7426

Agricultural Museum of Merced County
4498 E. Hwy. 140
Merced, CA 95340
209/383-1912

CHAPTER 7

San Luis National
Wildlife Refuge

Certain television programs transport viewers to various times both past and future. Without benefit of television you can step back in time about 150 years by visiting the **San Luis National Wildlife Refuge,** located about ten miles northeast of Los Banos. This 7,340-acre refuge was established in 1966 under the Migratory Bird Conservation Act and financed by duck stamp funds.

An agency brochure observes: "Few areas in California's San Joaquin Valley retain the flavor of early settlement days, when wildlife was abundant, the air fresh, and the landscape pleasant and pastoral. San Luis National Wildlife Refuge is such a place, a remnant of past times contrasting with today's great cities, crowded highways, and mechanized farmlands. Located within a few hours' drive of over six million people, this refuge promises to become one of the most important wildlife viewing and conservation education sites in the country."

You can expect to view principally migratory waterfowl. The San Joaquin Valley has been an extremely important stopover and wintering area for ducks, geese and cranes from time immemorial. Now the area suitable for the birds is radically diminished, and government refuges such as this one are critical for their survival. With bird parking lots limited, concentrations of the waterfowl are great. The three National Wildlife Refuges in Merced County offer winter sanctuary to roughly a half million birds, particularly pintail, green-winged teal, shovelers and mallards.

You may not be a bird fancier at all. Fine. How about mammals? The refuge provides homes for skunks, badgers, muskrats, long-tailed weasels, opossums, raccoons, coyotes, California ground squirrels, cottontails and black-tailed jackrabbits; which is all well and good except that none of these creatures is a big publicity seeker. Providing visitors with photo ops probably ranks last on their list of fun activities. You may do considerable looking and not see any at all. Consequently, I can't in good conscience urge you to make this trip just on their account. But I can urge you to go and see the stately herd of tule elk. Several dozen bulls and cows inhabit a 760-acre fenced enclosure, and every day of the year you are welcome to drive out between sunrise and sunset, take the 5.1-mile loop road around the enclosure, and elk-watch. While you may have to watch at some distance, the chances are good that some of the animals will be reasonably close to the road. Take your binoculars along in any case, and also your camera.

Calves are born in April and May. The herd has so prospered that occasionally some members have been moved to other locations. It surely must have been a sight 150 or more years ago to see perhaps thousands of these magnificent creatures roaming the Valley freely. Even to watch dozens roaming the refuge is something you will remember with pleasure. By the way, there's a wheelchair-accessible observation tower available. Visitors may want to stop and study the four interpretive panels which have been placed along the tule elk tour route, featuring information on the Yokuts Indians, tule elk management and riparian habitats.

Further Explorations

In addition to the loop around the elk enclosure described above, there is a second loop dedicated to bird watching, known as the Main Tour Route. If you like it, you may also want to drive over to the **Merced National Wildlife Refuge,** which offers another loop drive devoted to viewing waterfowl. With a good detailed roadmap of the area, you should have no difficulty in locating the Merced NWR and the best way to drive to it.

Best Time to Go

For bird viewing, October to May—or better still, December to February. A U.S. Fish and Wildlife Service brochure lists 204 species that have been observed on or near the refuges. The same brochure says that early morning and late afternoon are the best times of day for bird watching. Visitors are required to leave the refuge not later than 30 minutes after sunset. The refuges are open seven days a week year-round.

Nuts 'n' Bolts

From Highway 99 at Turlock or from Highway 152 at Los Banos, get on Highway 165 which connects those two communities. About ten miles north of Los Banos, turn eastward on Wolfsen Road. Now you have only about two miles to go to the San Luis National Wildlife Refuge entrance.

If your interest is largely limited to the elk, perhaps you'll be content with under an hour actually in the Refuge.

Key Contact

Central San Joaquin Valley National Wildlife Refuges
(Office location) 340 I St..
(Mail) P. O. Box 2176
Los Banos, CA 93635
209/826-3508

CHAPTER 8

Fresno: Love That Zoo and...

Happiness is . . . *what*, for you? The sentence has been finished many different ways. I'm going to nominate: "Happiness is a day at the zoo," or a few hours anyway. There's something intriguing about animals that makes coming close to them appealing for young and old alike.

So I have no hesitancy in urging you to find a day to get away to the **Fresno Zoo.** With 15½ acres and some 700 specimens of mammals, birds and reptiles, it may be a tad short of world class, but it's an excellent zoo. Fresno can well take pride in it, and you and your family can visit it confident of a good experience. Credit a lot of the Fresno Zoo's excellence to the man whose name it now bears, the late Dr. Paul Chaffee, Zoo Director from 1965 to 1990. Dr. Chaffee gave acclaimed leadership to the zoo throughout his long tenure and deserves credit for the Zoo's mission statement: ". . . conservation of our world's wildlife . . . education of the public . . . research in wild animal propagation and management, (and service) as a recreation site for Central Californians and visitors to the area."

When you visit, pick up one of the free zoo maps. Then set out on the larger of two loops either clockwise or counter-clockwise. Give particular attention to the animals and birds on the outside of your pathway. Returning to your starting point, make a second loop concentrating this time on the animals clustered at the core of the layout.

Let me take a moment to share with you what was perhaps my single most enjoyable visit. I particularly looked for camera shots which would lend themselves to humorous captions. For instance, one picture was of a zebra, and to it I attached the text: "Expressly designed and produced for black and white photography." I photographed two galapagos tortoises, one literally on the heels of the other. I fancied the second one saying: "No, officer, considering the speed we're traveling, I'm not following too closely." I witnessed a llama, ears back, eyes blazing, shouting at an intrusive rhea: "Back off, big bird. I won't take any more of your lip, I mean, beak." An orangutan, with the smuggest expression I ever saw, inspired the caption: "I'm OK. Are you OK?" If you're a camera person, I recommend this as a light-hearted way to enjoy your visit. Your hometown paper might even run some of your pictures as a photo feature. It happened to me!

In the summer of '92 the Zoo introduced a special attraction: the Winged Wonders Bird Show. Performances were offered at 11:00, 1:00 and 3:00 daily except Tuesday. The Zoo director told me the birds were at their best for the first show. Since the response of the public was good, he anticipated the shows would be a feature of future summers. Make it a point to inquire.

The Zoo has, of course, an admission charge. It is open daily from 10:00 to 6:30, May through September, and 10:00 to 5:00 from October through April.

Further Explorations

Adjacent to the Zoo is a recreational area especially for children: Playland and Storyland.

A stop some readers may want to package with a Zoo visit is roughly 15 miles west of Fresno in Kerman: **Sun Empire Foods.** Your short tour starts out with several varieties of plain fruit which are soon transformed into candy. I loved the line in the *Motorland* article that introduced me to this place. Said author John Goepel: "It's probably possible to get fat just breathing here." Half-hour tours are usually available weekdays between 9:00 and 3:00. You are strongly encouraged to phone at least a day in advance and tell when you expect to arrive and how many people will be in your party. (See below for number.)

For other things to see and do in and around Fresno, write to the Fresno Convention and Visitors Bureau (address below.) One of the Bureau's suggestions is the 85-mile Blossom Trail, which takes you through interesting country east and south of the city. However, there are only a few weeks when it is worth taking, due to the shortness of the blossom season, so you should schedule this trip between mid-February and mid-March. Because prime blossom time fluctuates at least a little from year to year, phone the Visitor's Bureau for current counsel.

Some other Fresno area options:

• **Blackbeard's Family Fun Center,** 4055 N. Chestnut Ave., Fresno 93726; 209/292-4554. Includes, among other things, a batting range, bumper boats, miniature golf, picnic area, video arcade, water slides. Open daily at 10:00 a.m. Admission charge.

• **Clovis Lakes Water Park,** 11413 E. Shaw Ave., Clovis 93612; (about 7 miles east of Clovis); 209/299-4242. Contains a variety of exciting wild, wet rides. Seasonal. Admission charge.

• **Fresno Art Museum,** 2233 N. First St., 209/485-4810. Changing exhibitions of Mexican and American art. Open Tuesdays through Sundays, 10:00 a.m.–5:00 p.m. Guided group tours by reservation. Admission charge.

• **Fresno Metropolitan Museum of Art, History and Science** at 1555 Van Ness Ave.; 209/441-1444. Open Wednesdays through Sundays, 11:00 a.m.–5:00 p.m. Group tours by reservation. Admission charge.

• **Kearney Mansion Museum** and Park at 7160 W. Kearney Blvd. (about 7 miles west of Fresno); 209/441-0862. Features the restored home of "Raisin Baron" Theo M. Kearney, listed on the National Register of Historic Places, and set within a 240-acre park. Guided tours are given Fridays, Saturdays and Sundays, 1:00–3:30 p.m. Admission charge.

• **Meux Home Museum,** 1007 R St. at Tulare St.; 209/233-8007. This is a Victorian home built in 1888 by a Confederate surgeon. Docent guided tours are offered Fridays, Saturdays and Sundays, 12:00 to 3:30 p.m. Admission charge.

• **Woodward Park,** north of Fresno, near the San Joaquin River. A beautifully landscaped park and bird sanctuary of 300 acres, containing playgrounds and picnic areas. Of special note: the manicured gardens and colorful koi ponds of the Japanese Friendship Gardens.

Best Time to Go

When visiting the Fresno Zoo, avoid, if you can, afternoons of the hottest days of the year. Most of the animals will be inactive, and the temperature is apt to wilt you, too. If you dislike crowds, a foggy day in winter might serve you well. Spring and fall days are likely to be "the greatest!"

Nuts 'n' Bolts

Accessibility is a real plus. The Zoo lies immediately to the east of Highway 99, between Belmont and Olive, and is well-signed on the freeway. It occupies a portion of 160-acre Roeding Park.

Key Contacts

Fresno Convention and Visitor's Bureau
808 M St.
Fresno, CA 93721
800/543-8488

Chaffee Zoological Gardens
894 W. Belmont Ave.
Fresno, CA 93728
209/488-1549

Sun Empire Foods
1220 S. Madera Ave.
Kerman, CA 93630
209/846-8208

CHAPTER 9

Selma/Kingsburg: Celebrating the Long Ago and the Far Away

In this chapter, we'll focus on Selma and Kingsburg, two towns in southern Fresno County and near enough to the city of Fresno that many residents commute there.

Some years ago a friend moved to Selma from a metropolitan community. He said he worried in advance that there might not be anything to do, that he might be reduced to watching the raisins wrinkle. Well, the raisins are something to see all right, as I will note further on, but let us begin our outing with a stop at **Selma's Pioneer Village Museum.** Perhaps you've already glanced at it as you've sped by the north edge of Selma on Highway 99. Occupying about twelve acres, museum structures are distributed around an expansive lawn dotted with trees. I chose to walk the circle clockwise, and here is some of what I saw.

• **Unger Opera House.** San Francisco-born Charles Frederick Unger (1862–1926) opened an opera house in Selma in 1888. The building now in the Village is not the original, but it continues the tradition of offering the community live theater. A City of Selma publication asserts: "Today the Unger Opera House hosts many plays and concerts put on by the local 'Raisin Cain Players,' the high school drama class, and many of the elementary schools. The Unger Opera House also hosts Western dance classes, Arts and Craft Shows, photography displays, and many other art-related events."

• **Victorian House.** Built probably in 1904, this structure was for many years the home of bank president and mayor Manuel Vincent. It contains many articles associated with the early 20th century. In an upstairs bedroom there is an old book addressing a subject that seems to be of interest in every century, a volume in the Self and Sex series with the title, *What a Young Woman Ought to Know.*

• **Lincoln Park School.** Built in August, 1901, at the cost of $1,000, this 20' x 30' frame structure was the last remaining one-room school in Fresno County when it closed its doors in February, 1976. Note nearby the school bell that served from 1889 to 1958.

• **St. Ansgar's Lutheran Church.** Methodists often speak of traveling preachers; this was a traveling church. It began as a school building, was later floated across the Kings River on a raft, and gained its present name and appearance (steeple added) in 1912. Today some couples seek it out as a wedding venue.

• **Southern Pacific Depot.** Completed in April of 1887, the depot was the first structure to be moved to the Village site, on February 8, 1974. Presently, the Fresno Model Railroad Club meets at the station on the first, second and third Tuesdays of each month at 7:30 p.m. The club has a model railroad exhibit on the second floor, and even now you can see the work-in-progress on first Saturdays. Phone ahead to verify hours.

Pioneer Village has the "biggest buggy shed on the Pacific coast," a band stand, six horseshoe pits, and an old Conestoga wagon (a "Prairie Schooner"). I was astonished at the height of the wagon's rear wheels; they're nearly six feet in diameter! Liking growing things as I do, I was intrigued by the huge wisteria vine which offers shade over seven ten-foot tables.

The Village is particularly a legacy of Selman Art Gonzales (1896–1983). He was an untiring collector of early-day artifacts, and many items at the Village came from his personal collection. He lectured on local history to thousands of school chilren and was a driving force in the formation of the Selma Museum–Historical Society and the Pioneer Village project.

The City of Selma took over the operation of the Village in 1991, and presently it is open to the public (with admission charge) Mondays through Fridays from 8:00 to 4:00, and Saturdays and Sundays from 10:00 to 4:00. Phone 209/896-8918 to verify hours; there may be seasonal variations.

Ready to go on? Staying free of the freeway, simply head south from Pioneer Village on old Highway 99 (adjacent to the Southern Pacific Railroad tracks and named Whitson St. in Selma). In 4.7 miles you should make a left turn across the tracks on Bethel; continue ½ mile more and park in front of the **Sun-Maid Growers Store.** Don't be put off if you're not a grower, for a sign advises "Public Welcome."

A brochure available at the store tells the Sun-Maid story. Sun-Maid's roots reach to 1912 when a grower-owned cooperative was formed. Located initially in Fresno, the company moved to its present site a couple miles north of Kingsburg in 1964, where on 130 acres it built the "world's largest raisin processing facility." At its busiest, Sun-Maid ships up to 1,000 tons daily. It sells three-quarters of its total production within the United States and Canada, while the remaining quarter goes to more than 25 countries throughout the world. About 95 per cent of Sun-Maid's output derives from Thompson's Seedless grapes. If you'd like a look inside the plant, you need to become part of a group ranging from 10 to 50 people and make arrangements in advance.

At the store you can purchase yummy things to eat: raisins (of course!)—love those chocolate-coated ones—plus prunes, apricots, pecans, walnuts, pistachios and more. Soft drinks are available. There are also things to wear such as shirts, caps and aprons. The store is open Monday through Friday from 9:30 to 5:00.

Next? Go back out to old Highway 99—identified here as Golden State—and continue south toward Kingsburg. From Bethel to Draper St., Kingsburg's main business street, it's 2.3 miles. You can tell you've come to Draper Street when you see the old Southern Pacific depot with the Dala horse on top. (More on Dala horses in a moment).

The **Kingsburg** Chamber of Commerce has its office in the depot. Park nearby, step inside for some local literature, and then, if walking is no problem for you, set out on foot. Proceed down one side of Draper Street for three blocks, cross and return on the other side. When you get back to your car, you can boast that you've "done" Kingsburg (not all of it, of course, but the heart of the business district).

The walk lets you experience something of Sweden without making a trans-Atlantic flight. Kingsburg was founded in 1886 by Swedish settlers fleeing the cold of Michigan, and it is reported that in 1921 95 per cent of the residents were of Swedish background. Although the percentage of Swedes has declined, Kingsburg still advertises itself as "the Swedish Village." This is reflected in the architecture, the flags on the light poles, and the festivals (Swedish Festival, the third weekend in May, and Santa Lucia Festival, the second Saturday in December). It is expressed in the choice of Sunne, Sweden, as a Sister City, in the name of the high school teams, (the Vikings), and in the ubiquitous Dala horses—even at McDonald's! A Chamber handout explains: "The Swedish Dala Horse originated in the province of Dalarna, Sweden, and was hand carved in various sizes and enameled in bright colors. When crops were poor, the carved horses were sold in neighboring provinces to augment family income. You can augment a family's income today by purchasing a souvenir Dala horse from one of Kingsburg's gift shops.

When you've finished your foot tour, here's what you might do next: Drive down Draper Street five blocks until you have the large, brick First Baptist Church on your left. Turn left, tightly around it, and start up Sierra St. When you pass Memorial Park with its bandstand, give thought to returning on a Thursday evening in summer for a delightful, outdoor concert. For that concert evening, bring a folding chair or perhaps a blanket to spread on the ground, and get settled by 8:00 p.m. The concert season is short, usually lasting just six weeks beginning with the first Thursday after the Fourth of July.

Continue on Sierra St. until you get back to the Highway 99 freeway.

Further Explorations

In the event that you want to pack more into your day, I'll identify a few options for you. You can easily drive down to Visalia. From Kingsburg, Conejo exit, to Visalia, Mooney Blvd. exit, is 21.6 miles. Then 3.2 miles south on Mooney Blvd. will bring you to lovely **Mooney Park** with its stately stand of old valley oaks and the Tulare County Museum. Watch out that you don't bump into park closure (Tuesdays and Wednesdays at the time of my April non-visit).

Continuing on down Mooney Blvd. (Highway 63) toward Tulare you will come, opposite Tulare, to **"The Ritz,"** a recent commercial venture that features water slides (said to be the fastest in the valley), batting cages, a pizza parlor, etc.

If I were to single out one of the most noteworthy of special valley events, it would have to be the Farm Equipment Show held in **Tulare** the second week of February. It is the nation's largest, which makes sense when you realize that the two richest agricultural counties in the world are Fresno and Tulare. With museum buffs in mind, let me also mention the Tulare Historical Museum at 444 W. Tulare Ave.

Best Time to Go

While Kingsburg's Swedish Festival weekend in May merits special consideration, you really can enjoy what I've described above virtually all year. I'd dodge a day in which rain is expected or when temperatures might soar over 100 degrees F. Spring and Fall make excellent seasons for visiting.

Nuts 'n' Bolts

The distance from Fresno (Highway 99/180E) to Selma (Hwy 99/43 junction, also signed Floral) is 13.8 miles. If you're traveling from the south, the distance from the Highway 99/198 junction west of Visalia to Selma is 22 miles. For doing the things I've outlined in the opening essay, four hours is a reasonable time allowance.

Key Contacts

Pioneer Village
Location: 1880 Art Gonzales Pkwy.
Mailing address: 2301 Selma St., Selma, CA 93662
209/896-8918

Sun-Maid Growers of California
13525 South Bethel Ave.
Kingsburg, CA 93631
209/896-8000 (including inquiring about tours)

Kingsburg District Chamber of Commerce
P.O. Box 515 (1401 California St.)
Kingsburg, CA 93631
209/897-2925

Visalia Convention & Visitors Bureau
720 W. Mineral King Ave.
Visalia, CA 93291
1-800/524-0303; 24-hour Activity Phone: 209/732-2711

Tulare County Museum
2700 S. Mooney Blvd.
Visalia, CA 93291
209/733-6616

The Ritz
110 N. Mooney Blvd.
Tulare, CA 93274
Information: 209/685-8991; Reservations: 209/685-0322

CHAPTER 10

Hanford:
A Three-Century City

Do you recall Washington Irving's story of Rip Van Winkle? Rip went to sleep for a very long time—20 years! When he awakened, things had changed dramatically. I mention this story because I had a Rip Van Winkle experience myself with regard to the city of Hanford. When I visited there in April of 1993, I had been absent for about 14 years. Were there surprises for me!

I found Hanford to be a community with its feet planted firmly in three centuries: the 19th, 20th, and 21st. An attractive, growing community of about 33,000, Hanford is certainly in touch with the present. It obviously has the amenities you would expect of a thriving 20th century San Joaquin Valley community and Kings County seat, including a vital cultural life, good schools, and a full range of medical services.

But why associate it with an earlier century? Let me explain. Hanford was born in the 19th century, laid out in 1877, in conjunction with the arrival of the Southern Pacific Railroad, and it was named for a Southern Pacific paymaster, James Hanford. Quite a few significant 19th century buildings have been preserved and add charm and interest to the town today. Among others, I call your attention to the Kings County Courthouse, the Sheriff's office and jail building, and the Santa Fe Railway depot, all built in 1897. In many places structures such as these would have met with the wrecking ball by now, but not here.

The Courthouse, in use as such until 1975, has been

creatively converted into a venue for half a dozen businesses. The old jail, La Bastille, now houses a restaurant and bar. The depot was beautifully remodeled in 1992 and now embraces offices of Amtrak, a bus company, and the Chamber of Commerce and Visitor Agency. The Visitor Agency has a free brochure which will enable you to identify a number of other 19th century structures. So the city gladly affirms its past and rejoices in its history.

I link Hanford with the 21st century because when you look around you think: here's a place that's ready for the year 2000. Consider, for example, the city swimming pool complete with water slide. Beautiful and heavily used in its initial season, 1992, the pool should serve well far into the future. Then there's the new 142,000-square-foot Hanford Mall, opened in March of 1993. Located at 12th Avenue and Lacey on the west side of town, it contains Gottschalk's, Mervyn's and Penney's, an eight-screen movie complex, a food court and about two dozen other retail businesses. Add to all that clean public restrooms, abundant parking, and a nearby Wal-Mart store. On the southern edge of the city you have Kings Industrial Park. The local Redevelopment Agency has been proactive in wooing corporations to this attractive industrial location, positioned almost midway between San Francisco and Los Angeles, and lots of good-looking houses are rising—highly liveable homes for the 21st century.

Now surely you understand my positive appraisal of this community, which in 1985 was the recipient of the prestigious Helen Putnam Award for Excellence, given annually by the California League of Cities. Having encouraged you to visit Hanford, let me specifically identify six things to include on your "to see" list.

1. **Civic Center Park.** I've already mentioned the historic Courthouse and Jail. The park also encompasses the Civic Auditorium (1924), the Veterans Memorial Building (1925), kiosks housing a florist, a hot dog vendor and a shoe shine man, a rose garden and a 1920s vintage carousel. The carousel was brought over from Visalia's Mooney Grove amusement park in 1982. Usual operating hours are Saturdays and Sundays from noon to 3:00, April through December.

2. **Superior Dairy Products Company.** It's across the street from the east side of Civic Center Park at 325 N. Douty St. A Hanford fixture for more than six decades, it is sought out by folks from a wide area for made-on-site ice cream. This is ice cream you will remember, tell your friends about, and go back for more.

3. **Hanford Carnegie Museum** at 109 E. 8th St. You won't even need to repark your car because it's only about a block and a half from Superior Dairy. The Museum is housed in the former public library, a 1905 gift of Andrew Carnegie and listed on the National Register of Historic Places. It has been a museum since 1972 and is open Tuesday through Friday from 12:00 to 3:00. Donations are encouraged but there is no set admission fee.

You can spend a swiftly passing half hour (or more) here viewing items dating back to the Native Americans who dwelt in this area long before Euro-Americans ever entered the Valley. Many other items reflect life in the Valley in the very early 20th century. Writers may take a fancy to a typewriter used by war correspondents during World War I, a far cry from the Macintosh on which I'm keying in these words. I was intrigued by the display of 29 wood plates and decided that the mulberry, cedar and scrub oak were my favorites.

4. **China Alley and the Taoist Temple** (1893). China Alley is located between Green and White Streets, just north of 7th. The Temple is another local building dignified by listing in the National Register of Historic Places. For a look inside it's necessary to make arrangements in advance—a point which will occasion further comment in a moment. I found I could walk here from the Carnegie Museum in under ten minutes, a distance of about 3½ blocks.

5. **Fort Roosevelt Science Center,** Davis & Grant Sts. (west of 11th Ave., behind Roosevelt School, .9 mile from the Amtrak station). The Center is particularly a mecca for children. School groups, scout troops, day care groups, etc. pour through to the extent of over 30,000 visitors a year. Principally, here's what they see: a small natural history museum housed in the relocated Southern Pacific freight depot, a covered wagon, a windmill, a cactus garden, a pond, a picnic area, and a log cabin. You'll observe wildlife undergoing rehabilitation, some of which

cannot be released back into the wild. On a visit you will likely see turtles, raccoons, peacocks, coyotes, ducks, chickens and more, while an on-site facilitator ensures that visitors not only see but also understand. About 50 nights a year groups actually stay overnight in the log cabin, which features a fireplace and an 1880 wood stove. How much they sleep I can't say, but reportedly they have a great time.

People of all ages enjoy the Center, but arrangements for a visit must be made in advance. Staff is very limited and demands on their time heavy. The center requests donations of $1 per child and $1.50 per adult.

6. **Kings Art Center,** 605 N. Douty St., open daily except Monday from 12:00 to 3:00. The attractive Center features a gallery with a show that typically changes once a month. A brochure outlines a whole year's program of exhibitions and makes mention of another important aspect of Center life: classes, lectures, demonstrations and workshops are offered in such disciplines as painting, watercolor, printmaking, photography, clay/sculpture, and papermaking. Visitors may wish to budget at least a half hour here during their day in Hanford. No admission charge; donations requested.

Perhaps the reader is wondering: how can I take all this in? You can do it easily by car. One parking will serve for stops 1, 2 and 3 above, while you may want to drive to 4, 5 and 6. But here's another idea I commend to you. Assuming you're starting your trip from the Fresno area or further upstate, avail yourself of Amtrak. Put a railroad experience in your day. From Fresno the roundtrip (1993 quote) is $11 (less for folks over 62).

When you reach Hanford, the Visitor Agency will help you see the sights. At the time of writing they were assisting about 2,000 people a month. They offer a unique shuttle service that meets incoming Amtrak trains with a canopied, remodeled fire engine (No. 1), a 1950 Studebaker. It will seat 15 adults at a time; with kids on laps the upper limits are a little indistinct. The driver will likely sound the siren, so folks will notice that you've come to town. The shuttle can be chartered at other times for a charge, but the Chamber of Commerce offers this service free on Fridays and Saturdays.

My recommendation is that you write the Hanford Visitor

Agency at least *two weeks in advance* of your trip. It would be ideal if you could link up with several friends to form a small tour group. Indicate what you wish to include in your day, and let the agency make local arrangements and smooth the way. Without advance planning and local help, you are apt to waste considerable time and perhaps be unable to visit certain places. For example, on the day of my visit, the two principal tour guides at the Taoist Temple were both occupied elsewhere, and I couldn't get in. You can save yourself my frustration by using the good services of the Visitor Agency.

If you're traveling by Amtrak, here are your parameters. Scheduled arrival time is 11:48 a.m.; you may head back toward Fresno at 4:33 or 8:03 p.m. Rail travel can work well, too, for folks coming up from Bakersfield. Be sure to verify times, for they are subject to change.

The 8:03 departure will allow an early dinner in Hanford, and there are many good options available to you.

Further Explorations

If you want to explore the town in greater depth or with more leisure, consider an overnight. The Visitor Agency will be happy to advise you regarding motel, inn or bed and breakfast reservations.

Best Time to Go

You could have a very satisfactory day in Hanford any time of year. To reduce the possibility of an especially hot or wet day, I recommend a spring or fall visit. There are many cultural events scheduled throughout the year, and a 24-hour toll-free events number is available to inquire about them: 800/722-1114.

Nuts 'n' Bolts

From the Highway 99/43 junction in Selma I found the distance to the Kings Art Center to be 17.7 miles, just over a 20-minute drive. Coming to Hanford from the Highway 99/198 junction west of Visalia, figure 14 miles and a little under 20 minutes. There's easy access also from the I-5/Highway 198 intersection at Harris Ranch.

Key Contacts

Visitor Agency
200 Santa Fe Ave., Suite D
Hanford, CA 93230
209/582-0483

Fort Roosevelt Science Center
(Behind Roosevelt School at Davis & Grant)
P. O. Box 164
Armona, CA 93202
209/582-8970

Kings Art Center
P. O. Box 376
Hanford, CA 93232
209/584-1065

CHAPTER 11

Bakersfield/Kern County: Proud Center of the Southern San Joaquin

What is it about human nature? You paint a line, and almost at once you find people who are determined to step over it. In this book I've painted a line of sorts. In order that people might not be confronted with driving inordinate distances, I've drawn that line around the geographical center of California at Oakhurst, and I've largely limited myself to destinations within a radius of 100 miles. But you can't put "San Joaquin" in a title and fail to reach out and embrace one of the Valley's most significant cities, so I'm inviting you now to be unrestrained. Indulge your human nature. *Step across that line!* If your orientation is upstate, head south. Take a couple of days for a feast of fine sightseeing opportunities. In this instance I'm going to set the food—the sightseeing options—all out on the dining room table and invite you to serve yourself— liberally—whatever you like! If you want to eat dessert before soup or salad, be my guest.

  • **California Living Museum,** P. O. Box 6613, Bakersfield, CA 93301; 805/395-1201. Here you'll find a 13-acre zoo, botanical garden, and natural history museum which features animals, plants and artifacts native or endemic to California. Open Tuesdays through Sundays 10:00 a.m. to sunset; closed Mondays unless a holiday. Directions: from Highway 178, head north on Alfred Harrell Highway approximately two miles to Lake Ming Road; right 100 yards to Frontage Road;

then left 1.5 miles to the museum.

• **Cunningham Memorial Art Gallery,** P.O. Box 1911, Bakersfield, CA 93303; 805/323-7219. This is Bakersfield's municipal art museum, featuring a permanent collection of paintings centered on California artists. Seven exhibitions a year add variety to what's there all the time. Open: Tuesdays–Saturdays, 10:00 a.m.–4:00 p.m., Sundays 12:00–4:00. Admission charge. Directions: from Highway 99, exit Highway 178 through Bakersfield (becoming 23rd St.). Turn right on M St.; turn left on 21st; follow 21st to R St./Central Park. The museum is in the park on R St. between 19th and 21st.

• **Kern County Museum,** and, next door, the **Lori Brock Children's Museum,** 3801 and 3803 Chester Avenue, respectively, Bakersfield, CA 93301.

Kern County Museum is an interdisciplinary museum of art, science, history, natural history and culture for Kern County. It includes a 14-acre outdoor museum with 60 buildings representing aspects of county life from the 1860s to the 1940s. Phone: 805/861-2132. Open: Monday–Friday, 8:00 a.m. to 5:00 p.m. (Ticket office closes at 3:00). Closed Thanksgiving, Christmas and New Year's Day.

The Lori Brock Children's Museum is a hands-on participatory museum geared for children between the ages of 3 and 12. Displays and activities in the areas of art, science, community awareness, technology and performing arts beckon the visitor. Phone: 805/395-1201. Open: Monday–Friday, 1:00–5:00 p.m. Saturdays, 10:00–4:00. School groups Monday–Friday, 9:30 a.m.–12:30 p.m. by reservation only. Admission charge.

Directions to both of the above: from Highway 99, take the Hwy.178 East/Hwy. 58 West exit and go east on 24th St. to Chester Ave. Proceed north on Chester through the Garces Traffic Circle to 38th and Chester.

As you make your way up or down Highway 99, you may wish to turn aside to see:

• **Delano City Heritage Park,** 330 Lexington St., Delano, CA 93215; 805/725-6370. Here you'll find a cluster of historic buildings, including the 1890 Wong House, the 1916 Jasmine School, the 1876 Jail House, the 1876 Valencia Adobe Replica, the 1888 Victorian Weaver House, and the 1890 Homesteader's

Cabin. Also in the park: a large display of farm equipment. Open: first and third Saturdays from 10:00 a.m. to 4:00 p.m., and by appointment. Phone 805/725-6370 or 725-9657. Directions: from Highway 99, Woollomes Ave. offramp, then east ¼ mile to Lexington St.; take Lexington St. north ½ mile. Museum on right (corner of Lexington St. and Garces Hwy.).

• **Minter Field Air Museum,** Rt. 11, Box 626, Bakersfield, CA 93312; 805/393-0291. Minter Field was a World War II U.S. Air Force training base, and the museum is housed in the original fire station. The collection includes World War II and Korean War vintage aircraft, vehicles and artifacts. Open: Saturdays and Sundays, 10:00 a.m.–4:00 p.m. Directions: from Highway 99, take the Lerdo Highway exit and go west approximately one mile. Minter Field is on the right side of Lerdo Highway; the Air Museum is located in the middle of Minter Field.

• **Shafter Depot Museum,** P.O. Box 1088, Shafter, CA 93263; 805/746-1557. The depot was built in 1917 and is listed on the National Register of Historic Places. It now contains local history, farm equipment, and railroad exhibits. Open: first Saturday of each month, 10:00 a.m.–2:00 p.m., other times by appointment. Directions: located on Highway 43 (Central Valley Highway) seven blocks north of Lerdo Highway. From Highway 99 drive west six miles; from Interstate 5 drive east 15 miles.

Three more attractions:

• **Antiques.** Available from the Bakersfield Visitors Bureau is an Antique Shops Guide which will help you locate over two dozen outlets in the vicinity.

• **Kern River Tours,** P.O. Box 3444, Lake Isabella, CA 93240; 619/379-4616. The Kern River is reputed to offer some of the most exciting whitewater in the state. Kern River Tours is appealing partly because of the range of trips offered: one hour to three days! It follows that the cost factor covers quite a range, too.

• **Mesa Marin Raceway,** P. O. Box 6217, Bakersfield, CA 93386; ticket office phone: 805/366-5711, Monday–Friday, 9:00 a.m.–4:00 p.m. The extensive menu of stock car races extends from the end of March to the middle of October. Write or phone for the current year's schedule. Throughout most of the season the races start at 8:00 p.m.

Hungry? Bakersfield has some fine places for you to dine. Have a great trip!

Key Contact

Greater Bakersfield Convention & Visitors Bureau
1033 Truxton Avenue
Bakersfield, CA 93301
805/325-5051

Chapter 12

Shadow Cliffs Lake
· Del Valle Lake,
Alameda County

Already I've outlined eleven day-trips up and down the Central Valley, Sacramento to Bakersfield. In this section, I'll describe five destinations a bit to the west of the Valley, again traveling north to south. I begin with two units of the East Bay Regional Park District, one "out back" of Pleasanton, the other "out back" of Livermore. Both towns are situated roughly halfway between San Francisco and Stockton.

Not only in California but almost everywhere, people are drawn to water. Have you noticed how towns and cities are located? Over and over again, they are sited beside the sea, or a lake, or a river. Illustrations abound: San Francisco, Chicago, St. Louis. And the point applies here, for the two parks under consideration thrive because of their wonderful water.

Consider first the **Shadow Cliffs Regional Recreation Area,** a mile east of downtown Pleasanton. The centerpiece of this 249-acre park is an 80-acre lake that lends itself to lots of activities: swimming, fishing, boating, windsurfing. The lake supports trout, catfish, blue gill and black bass. In another sense it supports a variety of boats: row, electric motor and paddle. Boats may be rented on site, and boats under 17 feet can be brought in, but no gasoline engines are permitted.

There's still more to be told about water here. Shadow Cliffs features a four-flume water slide, in operation daily throughout the summer and weekends in late spring and early fall. Toward the back of the park there's a levee, and beyond it more water, a chain of small lakelets where swimming and boating are not allowed but along which an adjacent trail makes walking a pleasant exercise. Waterfowl often enliven the views here.

Now let's turn our attention to **Del Valle Lake,** near Livermore. Water is the majestic and magnetic centerpiece of this regional park as well. At the heart of the 4,500-acre recreational area lies a five-mile-long lake, created by a dam. Swimming, fishing, boating and windsurfing are all available, just as they are at Shadow Cliffs. Here I can also point out more land-based options. At Del Valle you can ride bikes and horses, study nature, practice photography, hike, picnic and camp, all pursuits that become more enjoyable with the lovely lake in view!

A variety of types of boats can be rented on site, with a 10 m.p.h. speed limit in effect on the entire lake. Two beaches are strictly reserved for swimming. Changing facilities stand close by, and life guards guard lives in the summer. Even when the guards are not on duty, you may still swim in the designated areas during daylight hours.

Both parks possess great appeal. To buttress the point I need only to cite their visitation figures. In 1991, for instance, Shadow Cliffs drew 270,027 and Del Valle drew 466,796! Go ahead, swell the count. I think you'll feel well-rewarded by doing so.

Further Explorations

If you live in the southern section of the San Joaquin Valley, you might want to graft a visit to these parks onto a trip to the Bay Area for some other purpose. Just give yourself some extra time, coming or going, and at least do a reconnaissance. On my visit I lacked time for all the water things I've talked about. I enjoyed my stops anyway, and I believe you will, too!

For information on any of 48 parks and 11 regional trails that dot Alameda and Contra Costa Counties, contact the park district office.

Best Time to Go

Both parks are open all year. They look their loveliest in mid-spring. Fresh green foliage abounds, and such wildflowers as poppies and lupine brighten the landscape. Canada geese added to my own enjoyment of Shadow Cliffs on my early April visit.

Both parks count November to February the off-season, when visitation is light. From March to November—and especially during the summer—patronage runs from strong to overwhelming. Perhaps the most important thing to say here is when not to go: holiday weekends such as Memorial Day, Labor Day, and most especially the Fourth of July—forget it! Unless you're an early bird, you could find yourself turned away at the gate.

Nuts 'n' Bolts

Shadow Cliffs: From the I-580/N. Livermore intersection, proceed west on the interstate 5.5 miles to the Santa Rita Road exit at Pleasanton. Head south for 1.8 miles, being alert to make a left turn onto Valley. Valley will take you to Stanley. Turn left again, and very soon you'll see the park entrance on your right.

Del Valle: Let's suppose you're coming from the San Joaquin Valley (through Tracy maybe, or up I-5) and heading toward San Francisco on I-580. At Livermore, take the N. Livermore exit and head south. In Livermore itself, the street changes from being designated N. to S., and shortly to Tesla Road, but just keep going from the freeway a total of 3.8 miles. Turn right on Mines Road. Continue on Mines 3.6 miles at which junction point Del Valle Road goes straight ahead and ascends a hill beyond which lies the lake. This final stretch (to the bridge across the upper reaches of the lake): 3.8 miles. So, from the freeway to the lake, we have a total distance of 11.2 miles and a driving time of 20-25 minutes.

Key Contact

East Bay Regional Park District
2950 Peralta Oaks Court
P. O. Box 5381
Oakland, CA 94605
510/635-0135
For direct phone access to Shadow Cliffs, dial 510/846-3000, and for Del Valle information, call 510/373-0332.

CHAPTER 13

San Joaquin Valley National Cemetery

Let the story begin with the Civil War while Abraham Lincoln was in the White House. The President wrote a letter to a Mrs. Bixby in Boston, Massachusetts, which said:

> I have been shown in the files of the War Department a state-ment of the Adjutant General of Massachusetts that you are the mother of five sons who have died gloriously on the field of battle. I feel how weak and fruitless must be any words of mine which should attempt to beguile you from the grief of a loss so overwhelming, but I cannot refrain from tendering to you the thanks of the Republic that they died to save. I pray that the Heavenly Father may assuage the anguish of your bereavement, and leave you only the cherished memory of the loved and lost, and the solemn pride that must be yours to have laid so costly a sacrifice upon the altar of freedom.
>
> Yours very sincerely and respectfully,
> Abraham Lincoln

When I learned that the San Joaquin Valley National Cemetery in western Merced County was to be dedicated on Friday, June 5, 1992, I resolved to attend. And so I did, along with more than a thousand others. San Joaquin Valley National Cemetery! Here's a great place to meditate on the subtleties of war and peace and to appreciate the sacrifices that veterans and their families have endured to secure our country's goals. Remember with gratitude!

The cemetery is beautifully sited. Nestled in the hills of the Diablo Mountain Range about four miles out of Santa Nella at the end of McCabe Road, it exudes serenity and solitude. Particularly from the hill surmounted by a tall flag pole, you can enjoy a fine view which includes the O'Neill Forebay, just east of San Luis Reservoir. Right on site, a reflecting pond has been created down-slope from the attractive administration complex. Impressive plaques celebrate each of the armed services and the Department of Veterans Affairs.

I learned that this 322-acre cemetery became the 114th under the administration of the National Cemetery System, the sixth in California and the first in the Central Valley. It is planned to accommodate about 100,000 gravesites and to remain operational until at least 2030. It has a huge constituency to serve, with about 2.8 million veterans in California alone, which is over 10 percent of the national veteran population.

At the time of dedication resources were still being sought for an "avenue of flags." When all the flags are in place, the effect will be stunning. On dedication day the 50 state flags and the 26 or so national emblems in place evoked my patriotic spirit. Not only did they claim the attention of the eye, but also the ear, for a strong wind set all the flags to singing in chorus. (A fair few hats were lifted off heads, too!)

The official program especially credited those who gave the site: "The land for this cemetery was donated to the Department of Veterans Affairs by the Romero Ranch Company, Warren Wolfsen, President, on February 3, 1989." Since 1929 the Wolfsens have specialized in raising cattle for beef and dairy operations, as well as growing cotton and tomato crops.

The Cemetery's open hours are from sunrise to sunset. Whenever you go, remember to give consideration to persons who may be attending graveside services, and, if you have a pet along, respect the rule that pets must remain confined to vehicles.

Have we the capacity to make a sudden change of mood? I want to suggest that you engage fully your powers of observation as you drive to and from the Cemetery. See how many different agricultural crops you can identify. I listed ten on my trip—a number you should be able to exceed.

California farms produce so amazingly much. I never appreciated how much until the day (March 11, 1981) I clipped an article from the *Merced Sun–Star* headlined: "California is leader in 48 commodities." The report ranked the State second in ten crops, third in five, and fourth or fifth in five more.

In alphabetical order the clipping listed the 48 crops in which California led the nation in 1979:

"Alfalfa seed, almonds, apricots, artichokes, asparagus, avocados, broccoli, brussels sprouts, cantaloupes, carrots, casaba melons, caulifower, celery, chili peppers, crenshaw melons, cut flowers, dates, eggs, figs, garlic, grapes, honeydew melons, kiwi, ladino clover seed, lemons, lettuce, lima beans, nectarines, nursery products, olives, onions, oriental vegetables, peaches, pears, persian melons, persimmons, pistachios, plums, pomegranates, potted plants, prunes, rabbits, safflower, spinach, strawberries, sugar beets, processing tomatoes and walnuts."

I found that an astonishing list. I'll tell you someone else the list would astonish if he were alive today: Lt. Gabriel Moraga. Moraga came over from the Monterey Bay area to explore the San Joaquin Valley in June of 1805. Remember we're talking about the Valley in which many of the crops listed in the article are grown. In his journal Moraga wrote that in his opinion the area was unfit for farming. How wrong can one person be? On the other hand, in the absence of water, Moraga may not have been far from the truth about this Valley.

Further Explorations

You could easily include in your day a stop at the Romero Overlook Visitors Center at the north end of the B. K. Sisk San Luis Dam (barely off of Highway 152). However, I treat this stop option more fully in chapter 16.

Best Time to Go

In the early spring when the hills have donned fresh coats of green. Aside from that consideration, go whenever you like. You have year-round access on an excellent two-lane road out of Santa Nella.

Nuts 'n' Bolts

For the reader who may not recall where Santa Nella is, these directions: Santa Nella is right on Interstate 5, not many miles north of Los Banos (western Merced County). McCabe Road, accessed a short distance east of I-5, takes you out to the Cemetery, a distance of four miles from Santa Nella.

Key Contact

San Joaquin Valley National Cemetery
32053 W. McCabe Rd.
Gustine, CA 95322
209/854-1040

CHAPTER 14

Los Banos Creek

Do you like to be in an exclusive group, more exclusive than, say, the U.S. House of Representatives with its 435 members? If so, this particular trip is for you because usually only 336 people a year can take it.

The **Los Banos Creek Reservoir State Recreation Area** is southwest of Los Banos and immediately west of I-5. The excursion is a combination boat trip and hike which is offered on seven spring Saturdays and Sundays. Typically, the trips operate from the first weekend in March through the first weekend in May. Each trip is limited to 24 persons because that's the capacity of the boat. The boat trip portion — up Los Banos Creek Detention Reservoir — takes 30 to 40 minutes. That is followed by a 3.8 mile roundtrip hike along Los Banos Creek, a route that has been billed "The Path of the Padres" and leads to some rock-cradled pools in the stream.

The book *California Place Names* explains: "The creek took its name from the pools . . . called *Los Baños* (the baths) *del Padre Arroyo,* for Padre Felipe Arroyo de la Cuesta, who was at San Juan Bautista Mission from 1808 to 1833. According to tradition, he used to refresh himself in the pools when on missionary trips to the San Joaquin Valley." The stream was named for the baths, and in due course the town was named for the creek. Somewhere along the way the tilde (ñ) disappeared from over the "n" in Baños, but lately it seems to be making a comeback.

The treks to the baths are offered under the auspices of the San Luis Reservoir State Recreation Area and the Four Rivers Natural History Association. Rangers of the California State Department of Parks and Recreation escort the Sunday hikes, while trained volunteers accompany the Saturday outings. The leaders, besides piloting the pontoon boat, identify various plants and animals, tell of Yokuts Indian settlements of long ago, and touch on matters of more recent historical interest.

Let me share my experience with this trip, though your experience will probably be distinctly different because chances are you won't be rained on, as my group was. We encountered considerable rain on trail but were quite well prepared for it, took it in stride and enjoyed ourselves in spite of it. It certainly made the day special and memorable. Our problems came less from overhead than from underfoot. The ground along this trail makes the most slippery mud I've ever encountered. There was a stretch where every step we took was a challenge and an adventure. For several of us the seats of our pants offered ample evidence of our adventures!

At one point we passed a bluff with a major overhang. A natural respite from the rain, right? Wrong! Before we took shelter we looked up at scores of swallow nests, looked down at soil well fertilized by swallow excrement and decided a little rain on our heads was quite acceptable under the circumstances!

Perhaps our most captivating sight was five wild goats standing at the mouth of a shallow cave high on the mountainside.

During our lunch break — and there was a welcome break in the rain at lunch time — some us took a short, steep extension hike up a hillside on the north side of the creek. There, from a rocky outcropping, we viewed a vast expanse which may some day be a lake bottom, if plans go foward to build a huge dam, creating Los Banos Grande Reservoir. The reservoir would be capable of holding from 1.5 to 2.3 million acre-feet of water, although the size has yet to be set. For purposes of comparison, know that the present San Luis Reservoir, in the next drainage to the north, has a capacity of 2.03 million acre-feet.

Further Explorations

This trip departs from the boat ramp promptly at 8:00 a.m. Scheduled return is about 3:00 p.m. You probably won't want any fuller day than that.

Best Time to Go

Spring is the only time. In summer, the area is generally much too hot for enjoyable hiking.

Nuts 'n' Bolts

Perhaps the best route for persons coming through Los Banos is as follows: from the Highway 152/165 junction drive south one mile to Pioneer Road; turn right and proceed 4.1 miles to Canyon Road; turn left. Continue on Canyon Road all the way to the boat ramp area. Anticipate various curves in the road and a drive below the dam as you make your way to parking on the north side of the reservoir.

You will need a reservation. To secure that, phone 209/826-1196, Monday through Friday, 8:30 to 4:00, beginning the first Monday in February. If space is available, you will be asked to send a refundable reservation fee. One caller is limited to reserving four spaces; however, you can inquire about special group arrangements.

On the day of your trip, you will encounter a day-use parking fee.

You're advised to bring a minimum of two quarts of water per person, a lunch and good hiking shoes.

Key Contact

Department of Parks and Recreation
Four Rivers District
31426 W. Highway 152
Santa Nella, CA 95322
209/826-1196

CHAPTER 15

Pinnacles National
Monument

If our lives were measured in hundreds of thousands of years, I can imagine a writer of advertising copy extolling the **Pinnacles National Monument** with words such as these: *"See this spectacle while it's in your area. It's up from the south and on its way north. See it now while there's still time."*

Geologists estimate that about 23 million years ago the Pinnacles were down around Lancaster, some 195 miles southeast of where they are now, south of Hollister in San Benito County. In the far future they may occupy space that map makers now assign to San Francisco Bay. The Pinnacles are eroded remnants of an ancient extinct volcano, and they ride as passengers on the Pacific Plate as it grinds against the North American Plate, all the while bearing a course to the northwest. But don't bother to stand and watch. By human life standards, you've got lots of time. Nevertheless, I urge a visit to the Pinnacles the next time spring comes on your calendar.

They await you in a 17,000-acre National Monument established in 1908 by President Theodore Roosevelt. Activities in the park appeal to a variety of tastes. If you like to hike, you're offered 26 miles of trails. If wildflowers are your interest, you can search out and enjoy fully fifty species. Do you enjoy rock climbing? Many challenging surfaces are there for you, and you can get to them at times when the high Sierra rocks are virtually inaccessible. If you like camping, that's possible, too. Just outside the east entrance lies a private campground, and there's also an in-park campground. The problem is that the latter can only be accessed from the west, from Highway 101, and there's no road across the park.

Let's suppose you're simply a day tripper, that you're coming the 33 miles south from Hollister and using the east entrance. What should you anticipate doing and seeing? My advice is to go initially to the **Bear Gulch Visitor Center.** After looking over its fine relief map, set out along the Moses Spring Trail, which extends one mile, one way. (All this will make perfectly good sense to you when you have a National Park Service map in hand.) The trail will bring you to Bear Gulch Reservoir, a good place to enjoy a sack lunch. Heading back, use the trail through the Bear Gulch Caves. The National Park Service requires that you carry a flashlight for the caves, although a couple could probably share one.

Of the caves, one writer has offered this description: ". . . not like lava tubes: these are talus caves, places where numerous boulders have tumbled into ancient creek beds. They're not extensive and needn't be daunting. . . ." As you move through, be prepared to brush against rock walls and in the wettest of times to step into a tiny stream. At several points the passage way is very constricted. On a busy Easter Saturday, I was with a dozen or so folks going down the trail when we met a dozen or so folks coming up. For a short interval that seemed long we experienced gridlock. At length someone backed up a few feet, and we slipped past one another. The youth with me counted it "an adventure."

If you would like a longer, more physically challenging outing, I suggest climbing to the pass just north of Scout Peak. The distance one way is two miles and you gain 1,300 feet in elevation. (The Visitor Center's elevation is 1,260 feet.) The walk is rewarding both for its views of the area and for the lovely wildflowers you'll see if your timing's right. Bush monkey flowers were present in abundance when I was last up the trail.

Field guides, slides, flashlights and restrooms are all available at or adjacent to the Visitor Center. Before venturing out anywhere, do read and heed the "Information and Safety" section of your park brochure. Among the cautionary words you'll find there are these: "Carry one quart of water per person when hiking. . . . Be alert for poison oak."

Further Explorations

The Pinnacles National Monument park brochure lists many hikes. If you're spending a night in the Hollister area, a spring trip to the top of **Fremont Peak** (State Park) could be an excellent idea.

While you're touching **San Juan Bautista** anyway, you might enjoy a short stop at the old Catholic Mission and other historic buildings there.

Best Time to Go

Speaking of poison oak, it could be an excuse for a fall visit because it takes on such marvelous colors. By and large, however, spring's the time, when everything looks wonderfully fresh in new foliage. Green grass and wildflowers abound and nearly ideal temperatures prevail. Unless you want to settle down in a cave, summertime will likely present you with more heat than you can comfortably handle.

Nuts 'n' Bolts

From the northern San Joaquin Valley, what's required is driving over Pacheco Pass (Highway 152), picking up Highway 156, 8.4 miles north of Hollister and then proceeding down Routes 25 and 146 to the park entrance (33 miles).

From the southern San Joaquin Valley, you can access the Pinnacles by heading out of Coalinga on Highway 198, and then, after awhile, proceeding north on Route 25.

Key Contact

Superintendent
Pinnacles National Monument
Paicines, CA 95043
Phone: 408/389-4485

CHAPTER 16

From I-5 to I-5 via Highway 25: Beef, Oil, Fruit and Water

Don't you love loops? Do you dislike retracing your steps? I offer you a loop here along the western edge of the San Joaquin Valley, with I-5 defining one of its long sides. When you have a loop, two questions immediately arise: where do you enter it; and do you want to travel clockwise or counter-clockwise? You can easily access the loop at any of three points, depending upon your point of departure. From the northern end of the San Joaquin Valley, one excellent entry point is the intersection of I-5 and Highway 152 west of Los Banos. From the southern end of the Valley, you would start the loop at the intersection of I-5 and Highway 198 west of Hanford. From the west — that is to say from the San Francisco and Monterey Bay areas — Hollister provides a good point of entry. If you've visited the Pinnacles, you've driven one segment of this loop already.

My own choice was to begin the loop at **Harris Ranch** (just off Highway 198 immediately east of I-5) and to proceed clockwise. You may build a case for a different starting point and for the opposite direction if you like, but I'm going to write it as I took it.

Beef: Harris Ranch dates from 1937 when it was founded by Jack Harris and his wife Teresa. Leadership passed to the next generation in 1981 when John Harris and his wife Carole took charge. The ranch occupies a site roughly halfway (3½ hours) between Los Angeles and San Francisco.

I quickly formed a good impression of Harris Ranch, noting

the clean restrooms, the polished floors and the beautifully maintained grounds awash with the blossoms of poppies, pansies and marigolds. I said to myself, this is a fine place. I want to return when my wife can accompany me. She will like it! Some folks choose to access the ranch from the air, landing at the paved and lighted 2,800-foot airstrip. From the tie-down area it's a short stroll to the dining facilities and only a little further to the Inn — opened in 1987 — with its 123 deluxe guest rooms and Olympic-sized pool.

Diners have a choice of venues: the Ranch Kitchen, the Jockey Club, and the Fountain Court. In each, excellent beef entrees are much ordered. The company maintains a commitment to quality that extends beyond the beef to breads, pies and pastries, and some 33 agricultural crops raised on the company's extensive acreage.

If you want only gas and convenience store items, those services are there for you. If you want to throw a party for up to 275 friends and relatives, you could do that, too — in the Grand Ballroom.

Oil: Thirteen miles west of Harris Ranch is the western Fresno County town of Coalinga. En route there via Highway 198 you have a real treat: you pass through an oil field. You have never seen the equal of these particular oil pumps. In August of 1970 Jean Dakessian approached the local Shell Oil office with the idea of giving the oil pumps a little personality. Ultimately she painted 46: 23 for Shell and 23 for Standard Oil. A number of designs came by means of a community contest, and about a dozen folks whose entries were approved out of a total of 178 designs elected to build and paint their own creations. Good humor sprouted all over the oil field. Since most of the pump decorations featured animals, the collection was dubbed the "Iron Zoo," featuring an alligator, bull, butterfly, billy goat, crow, eagle, elephant, reindeer, turtle, zebra, and quite a few more. Wonderful! Already I want to return for another look. The zoo's fame has spread far and wide, with articles in the *Los Angeles Times* as well as the *London Daily Mirror*, which reaches an estimated six million readers. A community in Texas has flattered the zoo by imitation.

Coalinga itself is remembered by many San Joaquin Valley residents as the town that suffered severe earthquake damage on May 2, 1983. You can see a calling card left by the quake at the R. C. Baker Memorial Museum. In the rear—the annex—you can view a 65-ton oil pump that once worked at Mendota. The quake relocated it by 19 inches and caused it to punch a hole through the floor. I thought this sight alone merited the museum stop, but there was much else of interest: a mastadon fossil found in the nearby Kettleman Hills; a reed organ made in Connecticut about 1880; an intriguing exhibit of saddles, brands, bridles, bits and spurs. It's an excellent community museum, and it's located on the site that spawned the town's name.

The story behind the town's name is a surprising one and it runs something like this: In the late 1880's coal was discovered in this area. Since there was no railroad in the neighborhood, it fell to teams of mules to move the coal. In 1887, however, Southern Pacific built a narrow gauge line and established three coal loading points identified as Coaling Stations A, B and C. The coal supply was soon seen to be lacking in both quantity and quality and the mining stopped but, in the meantime, Southern Pacific had laid out a townsite adjacent to Coaling Station A. See where we're going: Coaling A . . . Coalinga! In 1889 it gained a post office. By April, 1906 it was an incorporated city.

The first functioning oil well was drilled in 1867, but the oil industry didn't really boom until quite a bit later. It got a great boost in September, 1910, when the Silver Tip Oil Company brought in a gusher. At the time it was accorded the title of greatest gusher in California with a flow estimated at 10,000 to 20,000 barrels a day!

If coal and oil were not sufficient claims to fame, Coalinga has a fine college: West Hills Community College, which features a hot air balloon festival the third weekend in November. The city also celebrates each Memorial Day weekend with a rousing Horned Toad Derby. The event traces clear back to 1934 and draws folks from far and wide, doubling the population from the usual resident 8,000 to around 16,000. Some 200 people may enter toads in competitions that race ten at a time. They begin when a barrel is raised from the center of the 16-foot diameter circle. The first toad to reach the edge of the circle wins the heat. Major excitement here, folks!

Today the town has rebounded remarkably from its sad state post-earthquake. Looking around, you see many handsome new buildings, older buildings repaired and repainted, and a sprinkling of tidy vacant lots where new structures may soon replace ones razed a decade ago. The Chamber of Commerce takes pride in the post-quake improvements made in the city's infrastructure, particularly the modernization of the water, sewage and gas lines and the undergrounding of the electric lines.

Leaving the town and its encompassing Pleasant Valley — still on Highway 198 — you encounter twists, turns and uphill pavement. At first the mountains appear virtually treeless, but soon you see rather diminutive junipers, and before long oaks and Digger pines. To me it seemed a pretty long 34.4 miles out to the Highway 198/25 junction.

I was surprised to find the next segment — to the turn-in to Pinnacles National Monument — also 34.4 miles. Along the road we saw lots of will-be-beef on the hoof. On the early March day of my drive, green grass flourished, but wildflowers were in shorter supply than I had hoped. Somewhere along Highway 25 we simply pulled off the pavement and proceeded to enjoy the lunches we had brought. For a view we overlooked a shallow, saucer-like lake about ten acres in area, one of several we saw along the way. For entertainment we counted passing vehicles. Do you suppose we witnessed the mid-day rush? Our total count: 7. We passed only one school. The Bitterwater-Tully School in southern San Benito County has one room (which can be divided), two teachers (plus one aide) and 30 students in grades K through 8. All except one child are bused to school. One wonders if it can have a future equalling its past: it was founded in 1874.

As you approach Hollister, the bucolic yields to "progress." You see well-tended vineyards, the venue for the San Benito County Fair, huge new homes in the Stonegate development, and then you're in the burgeoning San Benito County seat of Hollister, population 20,000 and climbing.

Fruit: From Hollister (Highway 25/156 Junction) 9.9 miles brings you to **Casa de Fruta** on Highway 152 (the Pacheco Pass road), several miles east of the Hwy. 156/152 merge. I remember stopping here in the mid-60s when it seemed little more than a roadside fruit stand. Three decades later it's a major development. Actually Casa de Fruta is a fourth generation family business founded in 1908. Today the basic farming operation and fruit stand are supplemented by fruit processing facilities, a bakery and candy factory, restaurant-coffee shop, gift shop, wine and cheese tasting room, 300+ space RV park, motel, swimming pool, Christmas tree farm, music hall and dance pavilion, one-foot gauge railroad, playground and a petting zoo.

On my last stop I particularly sought out the petting zoo. It's properly a magnet for photographers as well as children. I took away filmed images of a llama, a buffalo, and a Texas longhorn, plus memories of two baby goats only about 30 minutes old.

In recent years Casa de Fruta has moved decisively into special events. A folder I picked up detailed 23 events in twelve months. I'll mention five as examples: Easter Egg Hunt, Native American Pow-wow, Luau Under the Stars, Championship Dance Contest, New Year's Eve Party.

Water: If you begin your day trip fairly early and keep moving, you may be able to fit in one more short stop on Highway 152—at the Romero Visitor Center at **San Luis Reservoir.** (Be cognizant of the 5:00 p.m. closing time.) Distance from Casa de Fruta: 20.3 miles, all freeway.

At the Romero Visitor Center, besides viewing the dam and reservoir, you can learn a great deal about the building of the dam and other features of the California Water Project. A brochure provided these statistics: "The initial facilities . . . include 18 reservoirs, 17 pumping plants, 8 hydroelectric powerplants and 550 miles of aqueducts and pipelines."

The dam here—the B. F. Sisk San Luis Dam—can impound (when full) 2,038,771 acre-feet of water, making this the largest off-stream reservoir in the U.S. (Off-stream refers to a lake filled with water pumped from a source other than its natural watershed.) Much of the water comes from northern California via the Governor Edmund G. Brown California Aqueduct. It is pumped into the reservoir and stored for use as needed. At capacity the reservoir covers 12,700 acres. (Incidentally, an acre-foot of water translates to a little less than 326,000 gallons, approximately the amount of water an average family uses in a year.)

The energy consumption required to raise water from just above sea level in the Delta to over 3,000 feet crossing the mountains to southern California makes the State Water Project the largest single user of electricity in California, although its eight hydroelectric power plants produce enough electricity to reduce the Project's demand for energy by nearly half.

Further Explorations

For a comparatively short outing, you might consider doing (depending quite a bit on your departure point) either Romero Visitor Center and Casa de Fruta or Harris Ranch and Coalinga.

Best Time to Go

My own clear preference is spring. But if you can happily forego green grass, then fall can be fine. You could overcome my reservations about summer if you pick an atypically cool day.

Nuts 'n' Bolts

Most San Joaquin Valley residents will need to access I-5 either in the Los Banos/Santa Nella area or at the I-5/198 intersection (Harris Ranch). I used about seven hours to do the trip as described in this chapter, that is from Harris Ranch around to Santa Nella via Highway 25, a total distance I measured at 149.6 miles.

Key Contacts

Harris Ranch
Rt. 1, Box 777, Coalinga, CA 93210
800/942-2333

Coalinga Area Chamber of Commerce
380 Coalinga Plaza, Coalinga, CA 93210
209/935-2948

R.C. Baker Memorial Museum
297 W. Elm Ave., Coalinga, CA 93210
209/935-1914

Casa de Fruta
6680 Pacheco Pass Hwy., Hollister, CA 95023
408/637-0051

Department of Water Resources
31770 W. Highway 152, Santa Nella, CA 95322
209/826-0718, Ext. 253

CHAPTER 17

Indian Grinding Rocks, Daffodils and Other Delights

This chapter marks the first of seven explorations in the lower mountains to the east of the San Joaquin Valley, trips in the Mother Lode Country. In the early years of the Gold Rush it was rather widely believed that there was a huge vein of gold that extended all the way from the Middle Fork of the American River in the north clear down to near Mariposa on the south. What miners were at the time exploiting were thought to be mere off-shoots of this vast, still undiscovered "Mother Lode." Geologists have long since discredited the belief, but the designation of the area endures.

Moving north to south, our first suggested excursion—a loop of about 33 miles—begins at the Amador County seat town of Jackson, a community of over 3,500 located on Highway 49 at an elevation of 1,200 feet. Let us give our attention initially to one of my favorite places in the entire Mother Lode region: Indian Grinding Rocks State Historic Park, 1½ miles off Highway 88 east of Jackson.

Chaw'se: Here you'll find the site of a Northern Miwok village. Its most extraordinary feature is what I will call its acorn processing plant. In a flat limestone rock measuring about 175 feet by 82 feet, someone has counted 1,185 mortar cups, "the largest collection of bedrock mortars anywhere in North America," according to the official park brochure. About 300 petroglyphs (prehistoric drawings on rock) have been counted here, also. The mortar holes (*chaw'se* in Miwok) were not only a work center where food was processed but also a social center where tribal women kept caught up on the news of the day.

Not far from the *chaw'se* there's an impressive collection of about a dozen Indian houses (*u'macha'*) built largely of cedar bark. And near the dwellings stands an impressive Roundhouse (*hun'ge*), 60 feet across and 20 feet tall, built by Native Americans of the area in 1974. There's a game field for playing a sport with some similarity to soccer. Also on the site are granaries, called *cha'ka* and resembling large baskets, built to store acorns. All this occupies a lovely meadow punctuated with some of the most magnificent valley oaks you can see anywhere. On the day of my last visit (in early July), beautiful late-blooming wildflowers adorned the meadow marvelously.

On the eastern edge of the meadow, you'll find the Chaw'se Regional Indian Museum (open Monday–Friday from 11:00 to 3:00 and weekends from 10:00 to 4:00). It's a great draw for school field trips, housing an impressive collection of Indian baskets, a fine stock of Indian-related books for sale, many artifacts, and some informational panels on Native American life. A quotation from Willa Cather touched me: *"It was the Indians' way to pass through a country without disturbing anything; to pass and leave no trace, like a fish through water or birds through the air."*

If you want to get in touch with the heritage honored and preserved here, the best time to visit is the fourth weekend in September, when Native American families gather in large numbers and participate in dancing, hand games, singing and storytelling. Native American crafts and foods are available, and visitors are welcome.

The 135-acre park is at an elevation of 2,400 feet and is open daily from sunrise to sunset.

Volcano: When you bid your reluctant adieu to *Chaw'se*, turn left as you exit the park, and continue on the Pine Grove–Volcano Road a mile and a half to Volcano (population 85; elevation 2,053). Actually, there's nothing volcano-related here; it's just that the town's setting resembles a crater, wrapped all around by hills. I guess I'd call the hamlet quaint. In any event, it has an impressive cultural history. The first rental library in California was set up here in 1850, and four years later a little theater was founded by the Volcano Thespian Society.

As I strolled the main street, it was the jail, built in 1871, that especially intrigued me. I stepped it off and decided it was about 14 by 18 feet. Basically, it was a wooden box made of 1- by 12- inch timbers. On one side there was a rectangular break in the wood filled with a steel plate containing 36 half-inch-diameter holes. Perhaps it could pass as a window, but certainly it was the only ventilation system in sight. I'd say three or four hours would have seemed a very long stay.

Daffodil Hill: Now, let me say in my best tour conductor's voice, "Our next stop, ladies and gentlemen, will be Daffodil Hill." What we need to do is to drive eastward three more miles (Ram's Horn Grade). These are uphill and crooked miles, 20 to 30 m.p.h. territory, but the pines, oaks, cedars, madrones and manzanita make the ten minutes of curves very easy on the eyes.

To delight in Daffodil Hill's season of splendor, you need to think mid-March to mid-April. That's when you'll have the treat of seeing some 300,000 daffodils in bloom. A Dutch settler made a start on planting bulbs here back in the 1850s, and since the 1930s the McLaughlin family has vastly augmented the plantings. This generous family opens its six-acre garden to the public daily from 9:00 to 5:00 during the time when 25 percent of the flowers have begun to bloom until only 25 percent remain in bloom. There's no charge for entering these grounds; however, donations are welcomed.

When we say "flowers," daffodils aren't all we're talking about. Hyacinth, tulips, crocus, violets and lilacs are here, too. The *Amador County Visitor's Guide* reports: "Adding still more color to this Sierra wonderland are brilliant peacocks strutting amongst vintage farm machinery, rustic wagons and weathered buildings."

Sutter Creek: "Now, fellow tourists, let us go on to Sutter Creek." Simply drive west down Shake Ridge Road. Distance: 13.4 miles. Sutter Creek has a population of 2,000-and-growing. Among its interesting features is the Belotti Inn, built in 1860 and one of the oldest hotels in continuous use in California. If you're negotiating the sidewalks here, don't walk on automatic pilot because you might stumble on the stairs. Yes, sidewalks with stairs. If the stairs don't get you, watch out for the antique shops. You'll find a bunch, and I can imagine that they might reach out and pull some folks right in from the sidewalks. Or perhaps you're one to seek them out.

Anyway, all you need do to complete your loop is to drive about four miles south on Hwy. 49. Presto! Back in Jackson.

Jackson: Jackson evolved from a mining camp and is named for a popular early settler, Alden M. Jackson, a lawyer from New England. Its post office was established July 10, 1851. While you're here, you may wish to visit...

The Amador County Museum: It specializes in Mother Lode memorabilia, and some scale models relating to local mining activity are of particular interest. The museum is located atop a hill several blocks east of Highway 49. Address: 225 Church St. Phone: 209/223-6386. The museum is open Wednesday to Sunday from 10:00 to 4:00.

The Kennedy Mine Tailing Wheels: Visiting these wheels requires (from the Highway 49/Hwy. 88 intersection) a 1.4 mile drive out Main St. There were originally four of these monster 58-foot wheels that served to raise mine tailings a vertical distance of 44 feet per wheel until at last the wastes poured over a hill to be deposited behind an impounding dam. The wheels turned continously for 30 years.

The Kennedy Mine was one of the great mines of the whole Mother Lode region. Begun in 1856, it continued to yield gold until its closure in 1942. During its life span it grossed $34 million (in 1948 dollars). When it was shut down, it held the distinction of being the deepest mine (5,912 feet) in North America.

St. Sava's Serbian Orthodox Church: The church dates from 1894 and is the mother church of its denomination in the U.S. The picturesque white structure stands above Jackson Gate Road near the northern edge of town.

This further thought: Get a copy of the *Visitor's Guide to Amador County* from the Chamber of Commerce, 24 pages of data gathered expressly to help the likes of you. Take special note of the Walking Tours that are detailed for Jackson, Ione, Plymouth, Fiddletown, Drytown, Amador City, Sutter Creek, Pine Grove and Volcano.

Further Explorations

Consider giving the area parts of two contiguous days, or making single day trips at different times of the year, for example, March and September.

Best Time to Go

It's a tough call. *Chaw'se* summons you in late September; Daffodil Hill in late March. Aside from that, you could do this loop during any season, except that I wouldn't try to do it in the midst of a winter storm.

Nuts 'n' Bolts

Simply study a state highway map and choose a sensible route from where you live to Jackson. If you live in the lower San Joaquin Valley, I would encourage you to drive a stretch of Highway 49. The countryside offers more of interest than most valley miles do, and you'll probably like having a look at such recognizable Mother Lode names as Sonora, Angels Camp, San Andreas and Mokelumne Hill.

Key Contacts

Amador County Chamber of Commerce
30 S. Highway 49
P. O. Box 596
Jackson, CA 95642
209/223-0350

Indian Grinding Rock State Historic Park
14881 Pine Grove–Volcano Rd.
Pine Grove, CA 95665
209/296-7488

CHAPTER 18

California Caverns

If you're ever feeling it's too hot, too noisy, too bright, then pick yourself up and treat yourself to a visit to **California Caverns.** Here you can soothe your assaulted senses in cool, quiet darkness. These caves are located in Calaveras County, about ten miles east of San Andreas. Quiet and dark today (when tours aren't passing through), these caverns once resounded with a bustle of activity. Discovered by gold prospectors in 1849, and located near Cave City, a once booming gold rush town of two to three thousand, the caverns served as the site for a variety of events. Heated political debates once resonated through some of these chambers as Cave City Council members held their meetings. The coolness of the caves made "do-si-doeing and promenading your partner" at the local square dances a less perspiring experience. Some couples even chose the sanctuary of these seemingly eternal caverns as the place to declare their wedding vows.

The enchantment of these caverns, however, has extended far beyond the limits of Cave City. Names and places inscribed on cavern walls suggest that visitors came from such distant points as China and England. Bret Harte, Mark Twain and John Muir were among the notables who came to call. Muir was moved by his plunge into the earth's insides to say:

"When we emerged into the bright landscapes of the sun everything looked brighter, and we felt our faith in Nature's beauty strengthened, and saw more clearly that beauty is universal and immortal, above, beneath, on land and sea, mountain and plain, in heat and cold, light and darkness."

Cave City eventually succumbed to the same fate as many other gold rush towns. Virtually nothing remains today, except, of course, the caves, and they are reason enough to make the trip. Compared with other caves in the region, you have here a larger area open to the public, and parts of what you're shown are less disturbed by human hands. Portions of the cave system are still "alive," growing, in continuing process of geological formation. Besides the fairly conventional stalactites and stalagmites, you encounter gorgeous draperies, soda straws, and helictites, which have a peculiar ability to grow sideways and twist and turn like a helix or a "pig tail." One room in particular, the Jungle Room, was walled off and thus saved from the ravages of souvenir hunters.

For roughly three-quarters of a century the caves were little visited, but now that has changed. Since 1979 the caves have been owned and operated by the same family that owns Moaning Cavern at Vallecito. With good tours regularly offered and widely advertised, visitation has soared. Basically, visitors have a choice of two tours. The first carries the label "Trail of Lights." Suitable for the whole family, this 80-minute tour is substantially less strenuous and time consuming. Still, it preserves the inherent excitement of cave walking, taking you through constricted passageways, under low ceilings and into the untouched beauty of the Jungle Room.

Going into the Jungle Room—which you don't have to do—you may brush walls and pick up a smudge of dirt on your clothing. That should not deter you, but it could influence what you choose to wear. You will be lent a hard hat for your tour. And, as a six-foot plus individual, I will tell you that I "used" my hat a number of times!

For the more daring, there's the "Wild Cave" tour. This five-hour extravaganza is open only to healthy and adventurous adults and youths (aged 12 and over). The operators supply coveralls, gloves and a hard hat with a light. You supply a willingness to crawl and climb, wiggle and squirm—and to paddle rafts over deep lakes. You may take comfort in being in the constant care of highly trained guides. Previous caving experience isn't required. The operators do require, however, advance booking for this tour.

Other cave visiting possibilities are touched on in Chapters 24, 36 and 37.

Further Explorations

If you're coming up from somewhere south of San Andreas, consider using alternate routes, perhaps taking a stretch of Highway 49 one direction, and the county road running past Tulloch Reservoir and through Copperopolis the other direction.

You may wish, at the least, to stop for a meal in **San Andreas,** the Calaveras County seat since 1866. Calaveras is one of California's original 27 counties. It is named after the river, and for that give credit to the Spanish explorer Gabriel Moraga. On an expedition in 1808 he noticed a place along the river with some number of exposed skulls, hence he identified it as the river of the skulls (*calaveras* in Spanish).

It seems appropriate to comment here on where the name "California" came from. It has been traced to a novel by the Spanish writer Montalvo entitled *Las Sergas de Esplandián* (*Esplandian's Adventures*). Published about 1500, the novel depicted an extraordinary island realm, California, of which the queen was Calafia. The name was applied to what we now call Baja California, and for many years Baja was believed to be an island. There is speculation that an explorer named Fortún Jiménez named the peninsula in the winter of 1533, but this is uncertain. What can be documented today is that two maps made in 1562 designate the body of water touching the peninsula *Golfo de la California.* In the 18th century the Spaniards, wanting for themselves not only the peninsula but the contiguous land to the north, began to speak of *Baja California* and *Alta* (or *Nueva*) *California.*

Just down the road from San Andreas lies **Angels Camp,** celebrated in Mark Twain's famous story "The Jumping Frog of Calaveras County." The frogs are jumping still, especially the third weekend in May when the town hosts the annual Jumping Frog Jubilee in conjunction with the Calaveras County Fair. Both Angels Camp and San Andreas have museums you may wish to visit.

Best Time to Go

The operators of California Caverns warn in their brochure: "Due to high water from winter rains, California Caverns are sometimes closed *approximately* Dec.–May." During this period it is recommended that visitors phone first to find out if the caverns are open. The Trail of Lights tour is generally available from 10:00 a.m. to 5:00 p.m. daily throughout the summer, 10:00 to 4:00 during the fall, weekends only in November.

The Wild Cave tour operates daily from June to October (weekends in November), and departs at 9:00 a.m. Call at least a week in advance for reservations.

Nuts 'n' Bolts

Whatever road map you rely on should guide you to San Andreas on Highway 49. About a mile and a half south of downtown, Mountain Ranch Road branches off Highway 49 to the east. Take it. Continue on it for 8.5 miles, then turn right on Cave City Rd., and continue on it for about 1.5 miles. That will take you to your tour starting point, which, incidentally, is about a quarter of a mile from the cave entrance. Associated with the ticket office are restrooms, and opportunities to buy postcards, souvenirs and soft drinks. A couple of picnic tables stand close by, and you may wish to spread your lunch on one, either before or after your tour.

Key Contacts

California Caverns
P. O. Box 78
Vallecito, CA 95251
209/736-2708

Calaveras County Visitor Center
P. O. Box 637
Angels Camp, CA 95222
209/736-4444

CHAPTER 19

Riding Rafts on Rampaging Rivers

River rafting has been a popular recreation for quite awhile. Some professional outfitters began offering whitewater adventures in the late 60s. The 70s and 80s saw rather dramatic growth in the industry in California, although the early 90s witnessed a leveling-off attributable to the drought. Still, an estimated 280 to 300 thousand people here in northern California put rafting experiences into their summer of 1993. And they did it between April and September. Some rivers which have no regulation of water releases from upstream dams have much shorter seasons. Runs on the Merced River, for example, are largely limited to May/June.

Now you are faced at once with two decisions: what river and what river rafting company (about 50 possibilities). I beg to disqualify myself from offering you specific advice because I've only been on two rivers with two professional outfitters. This limited experience does not an expert make. So all I aim to do here is to encourage you to give river rafting serious consideration. And I want to do that by sharing with you a report I wrote about a two-day trip I made on the Merced River way back in 1983, a report published in the February, 1984, issue of *Yosemite.*

The title of our two-day rafting trip sponsored by the Yosemite Association was "On the River." Our party had been on the river about an hour when a quarter of the group—six out of 24—found that the title had missed the truth; they were *in* the river, unexpectedly ejected from two different rafts in the turbulence of Ned's Gulch.

Though the river was not (at that time) designated "wild and scenic" by the federal government, any rafter will assure you the Merced River is certainly wild. As a precautionary measure, we had stopped and surveyed the Gulch before running it. Even so, we sustained what I'll call non-injury accidents. I was in the lead boat with head boatman Jimmy Grissom manning the oars. Within several seconds of entering the white water our boat seemed to be standing on its left side and I thought it would flip over. It did not. The man on my left fell out—our sacrificial lamb, I guess—and the boat righted itself.

Grissom's voice rang out, "We've got swimmers!" Within seconds we were able to pull our gasping lamb aboard, and in short order five others who had spilled out of another raft. We gained a sense of community born of shared crisis. And more adventure lay ahead.

Our group had assembled the evening before. We were 18 in number, and joined by six more people the next day, quite evenly balanced as to gender, diverse as to age. The senior member of our group was a 65-year-old woman from Los Altos. Aside from our guides, she proved to be the most experienced rafter of the lot. Already to her credit were two trips on the mighty Colorado, one trip in Alaska and one on California's American River. She said that Quarter Mile Rapids, which we negotiated our second day, was as tough and exciting as anything she had encountered elsewhere.

On Monday morning at 9:00 we gathered at El Portal. There we made final decisions concerning what we could live without for two days, locked our cars, boarded a bus, and rode several miles down river. By now we were under the care of OARS, Inc. (Outdoor Adventure River Specialists), with whom the Yosemite Association had arranged the trip. At riverside, opposite Cedar Lodge, we found five river rafts, 16-foot inflatable Avon Professionals, awaiting us. We were briefed on river safety. We put such things as cameras and watches in ammo boxes which were tied down securely. Our sleeping bags and other personal gear would travel by truck to an appointed place down river. Most of our group were first-timers, and I was conscious of some anxiety as we pushed off from shore and were grasped by the water flowing at a volume of about 3,200 cubic feet per second.

Any worries we had were largely allayed by the fact that we were in the hands of skilled, experienced professionals. Grissom, for example, had been running rivers for five years, and had over 350 days on-river to his credit. I failed to ask him about his "in river" experiences. Some things it may be better not to know. Later in the year, he was off to Zambia where he worked the churning Zambesi below Victoria Falls.

Not only were the OARS staff members superb boat handlers, but ashore they proved to be excellent cooks. It seemed to me that every meal approached banquet proportions. On Monday night, for example, we grilled steaks over a wood fire at our beach campsite. Tuesday morning we were treated to a large omelette, fresh strawberries and cream.

After breakfast, we broke camp and ferried our plastic-garbage-bag-encased personal gear a short distance down river to where it could be loaded on a truck. We floated further toward the top of Quarter Mile Rapids. Here we stopped for over an hour. During that time our guides scouted the entire stretch of churning white water to which we would soon commit ourselves.

We made sure everything was tied down securely. Life jackets were a comforting requirement. Those with wetsuits felt especially well prepared for a possible repeat of the dunking of the day before. We appreciated the ruggedness of our $2,700 rafts and were glad to know that there were six separate air chambers, so that if one got a puncture, we would still remain afloat. A troubling question remained: could we negotiate such extended turbulence without getting separated from our rafts? Many of us admitted to a measure of anxiety about the answer.

My boat, the Grissom boat, led off. Icy water showered over us again and again. We wondered briefly if we were in a rodeo riding bucking broncos. Then, suddenly we took a sharp left into an eddy. We were through — safely! I couldn't believe how fast. Something like a bullet through the barrel of a rifle, I reckon.

We watched the following boats exit the white madness. A couple of boats emerged almost completely swamped, but they were quickly bailed out. One boat came in minus one crew member, but he was kicked out very near the river's edge and had made shore with no difficulty. Sighs of relief all around! Some hard work still ahead!

We found ourselves within about 50 yards of the upper lip of North Fork Falls. The falls are actually on the main river, but only a hundred yards from the confluence of the North Fork. The river drops roughly fifteen feet in a distance of perhaps 50 feet. "Unnavigable" is the firm opinion of sane raftpersons. So we faced portage time. We had to pull the rafts up to the old Yosemite Railroad right-of-way, hand carry them a hundred yards, and then lower them by rope into the river. A very considerable effort! By now it was 2:00 p.m., and time for a most welcome lunch.

The remainder of the trip was "a piece of cake." We ended our adventure by paddling along a far-from-full Lake McClure. We beached our boats and were bussed back to our cars at El Portal, though not without a stop. Yes, we had to make a from- the-road inspection of renowned Ned's Gulch. Did we really go through that? You better believe it!

Further Explorations

I don't feel qualified to recommend one river or operator over another. I simply wish you happy shopping and good rafting!

While our attention is focused on Sierra rivers, let me reveal how a number of them got their names. Moving from north to south, I'll cite first the **Stanislaus.** In 1827 or 1828 an Indian associated with Mission San Jose ran away. He had been given the named Estanislao, presumably for one of two Polish saints, both called Saint Stanislas. Estanislao was pursued by soldiers who were alarmed because they thought he intended to lead a general insurrection. They engaged him in a bloody battle along the river which later was given his name. John Fremont used the current spelling of the name on a document written in March 1844.

The name **Tuolumne** is believed to go back to a Central California Miwok tribe. The people lived in caves or recesses in rocks. The first part of the word, variously spelled, referred to their dwelling places. The -umne suffix means people or tribe in both the Miwok and Yokuts languages.

The naming of the **Merced** is a more assured matter. Gabriel Moraga's expedition came upon the river on September 29,

1806, five days after the feast day of Our Lady of Mercy. They named it *Nuestra Señora de la Merced*.

The comparatively small **Chowchilla** River seems to have gotten its name from a Yokuts tribe that lived along its lower reaches, a group called the Chauciles.

The **Fresno** River has borne that designation since at least 1851, and it is believed to have been named for the Oregon ash trees (*Fraxinus oregona*) which grew along it. Ash = *fresno* in Spanish.

Gabriel Moraga is credited with naming the **San Joaquin** in 1805 or 1806. Possibly he came to the river on about the feast day (March 20) of Saint Joachim, honored by Roman Catholics as the father of the Virgin Mary.

For a note on the Kings River, see chapter 36.

I am unaware of any raft trips on the Mokelumne River, but I want to comment on the name anyway. *California Place Names* says the name is "derived from a Plains Miwok village near Lockeford. The ending -*umne* means 'people' (as we have already noted), but the meaning of the specific term is unknown."

Best Time to Go

By way of generalization, I'd say late spring or early summer. The flow in some of the rivers gets too low as the summer wears on.

Nuts 'n' Bolts

Pick your river. Your principal options north to south are the American, Stanislaus, Tuolumne, Merced, Kings, and Kern rivers. Then there's the matter of choosing your professional outfitter. About 50 belong to California Outdoors, the outfitters' association. You can make contacts by calling the Association's toll free number: 800/552-3625. An alternate approach is to look under "River Trips" in the yellow pages of your telephone book. Look for brochures at Chamber of Commerce offices and motels. If you have friends who have made whitewater trips already, you may wish to take their counsel into account.

I think it makes sense to choose a less demanding stretch

of river before braving class III and IV rapids. I'd say further, go for a one-day trip before buying into a two-day outing.

Key Contact

California Outdoors
P. O. Box 401
Coloma, CA 95613
800/552-3625

CHAPTER 20

Hetch Hetchy

Awesome! There are degrees of awesome, and I think they can be illustrated along a stretch of the Tuolumne River canyon generally referred to as Hetch Hetchy and accessed from Highway 120 east of Modesto and Groveland.

Hetch Hetchy is principally an 8-mile-long reservoir created by a massive 312-foot high concrete dam—O'Shaughnessy Dam—built by the City and County of San Francisco. Construction began in 1914, and the dam was raised an additional 85 feet in 1938. Unfortunately, the dam precipitated the flooding of a valley which John Muir thought was nearly as marvelous as Yosemite Valley. In any case, the dam is there now. Parking is available immediately west of the dam. Go out to the middle of the dam and relish the view of the reservoir, and, on your right, Kolana Rock soaring 2,000 feet above the water. Turn the opposite direction and peer into the depths of the Tuolumne River canyon. Anytime of year I count all this "level one awesome."

It goes to "level two" when the reservoir is full, the spring run-off is high, and enormous quantities of water spill over the dam gates and surge with pent-up power through several pipes in the dam's face. Mist reminiscent of Niagara Falls fills the chasm below the dam, and usually you can find a vantage point for watching rainbows dancing in the mist.

"Level three awesome" is when the canyon wall beyond the reservoir is adorned in spring with two rampaging falls. The closer one carries the strange name Tueeulala and dries up before the summer gains much of a foothold. The second, Wapama, is on a much more substantial stream. I've seen it nearly dry at the end of a very dry summer, but I've also seen it bearing such a massive flow that you could not safely cross the bridges near its base. Moreover, the swirling mist will give you a free cold shower!

I like Hetch Hetchy! Can you tell? And I encourage you to go, even if you only stroll out on the dam. However, I hope you'll feel up to walking to Wapama Falls and back. Roundtrip, that's 4.8 miles, relatively level for the most part. Besides lovely views up and down the lake and canyon, you may find the trip richly embroidered with spring wildflowers. There's a nice variety which come to full flower over a span of several weeks: principally brodiaea, farewell-to-spring, monkeyflower, narrow-leaved mule's ear and mariposa lilies.

Another interesting feature of the walk is passage through the 500-foot-long lighted tunnel immediately to the north of the dam. About a mile into your hike, and after "uphill" has probably registered in your mind, you'll come to a trail junction. Bear to the right. This is the only place you could possibly go wrong. I encourage you to take a sack lunch to the base of Wapama Falls, and linger there a bit. Two and a half to three hours should be a correct time allowance from car to falls and back to your car.

You should not be bothered by elevation. When the reservoir is full, the surface is only 3,796 feet above sea level. Do realize that your hike could be pretty hot. Look out for—don't touch any—poison oak.

A note on the name: Hetch Hetchy is derived from a Miwok word of uncertain meaning. It may have been used to denote a kind of grass or plant with edible seeds. The name might have meant "acorn valley." Certainly there were lots of acorns there and they were much used by Native Americans.

Further Explorations

Let me mention two possibilities. If time allows, turn downhill at the west end of the South Fork (of the Tuolumne River) bridge. The bridge is east of the Rim of the World scenic vista and less than a quarter of a mile west of the Highway 120 junction with the Cherry Oil Road. Drive perhaps a quarter of a mile and enjoy a short stop at beautiful **Rainbow Pool.** If you've done the hike at Hetch Hetchy and the month is July or August, you might like to swim here. It's a lovely spot. If you don't stop on this trip, stop another time. (Warning: You may encounter a locked gate by the bridge. There remains the possibility of parking on a spur off the Cherry Oil Road and walking down to the Pool.)

The other possibility I list for the truly ardent hiker. If the 4.8 mile hike to Wapama Falls is entirely too tame for you, then perhaps you should set your sights on a 13-mile roundtrip jaunt to **Rancheria Falls.** Beyond Wapama Falls the trail is marked by a number of ups and downs, so over the course of the day, though your net elevation gain may be under 700 feet, you'll find that you've climbed closer to 2,000. Much of the time you may be in full sun and it could be hot. If you're in good shape, I'd recommend this hike to you. The day I did it, a companion failed to bring sufficient liquid, so three of us shared. By hike's end we were all water-less, and I hope never to be as thirsty again.

There are a couple of beautiful swimming holes associated with the Rancheria Creek series of cascades.

Best Time to Go

Press me to mention a single month, and I'll say May, largely because of the abundance of water and wildflowers.

Nuts 'n' Bolts

If you're coming up on Highway 120 from Oakdale, your shortest, fastest route is as follows: soon after the community of Buck Meadows (1.1 mile), you'll see on your left a vista point signed by the U.S. Forest Service "Rim-of-the-World." Do stop a few minutes and walk to the far end of the observation platform, then peer down to see an attractive waterfall on the South Fork of the Tuolumne River. Going on (1.6 mile), you'll soon cross the South Fork on a high bridge. Then in about a quarter of a mile on your left, you should spot the start of the Cherry Oil Road. Drive mostly uphill 5.4 miles, then turn right on the road to Camp Mather and proceed an additional 7.6 miles. Camp Mather is a summer recreation community maintained by the City and County of San Francisco. From Camp Mather to the dam: 9.1 miles. There's a Yosemite Park entrance station on this stretch. If you haven't already paid at another park entrance station, you may need to reach in your pocket for the prescribed fee here.

If you're traveling up from Yosemite Valley, exit the park at the Big Oak Flat Entrance Station, proceed 1.2 miles and turn right on Evergreen Road. A drive of 7.5 miles will bring you to Camp Mather.

Key Contact

Yosemite National Park (See Chapter 26)

CHAPTER 21

Mariposa: Mining and Minerals

Are you interested in gems and minerals and in how things were in the central Sierra foothills around 1850? If you answer "yes," then I recommend the trip to Mariposa very highly. By all means, wheel your way there, most likely eastward from Merced on Highway 140.

Let me suggest three stops:

1. **Mariposa County Courthouse.** From where Highway 49 (coming in from Oakhurst) merges with Highway 140 at the base of downtown, drive on up the combined Highway 140/49 to 8th, turn right one block, and then left a block and a half. There you are in front of "the oldest courthouse in continuous use west of the Rockies."

Mariposa means butterfly in Spanish. Mariposa County dates from 1850 when California was subdivided into 27 counties. At that time Mariposa County occupied more than one-fifth of the state's area, or approximately 30,000 square miles. Today the county contains a modest remnant of 1,455 square miles. The courthouse came along in 1854, and would you care to guess the amount of the construction contract? $9,000. The building has made the list of National Historic Landmarks "because some of the most celebrated and noted civil, mining and water cases were held in its courtroom." Of special interest is the clock in the tower. It was shipped from England around Cape Horn and installed in 1866. Associated with it is a 267-pound bell which still tolls each hour.

Tours of the Courthouse are usually conducted on Saturdays

and Sundays, 10:00 to 4:30, Easter to mid-October. If you visit Monday through Friday, you'll find a working courthouse, and your meandering will need to take that into account.

2. **Mariposa Museum and History Center, Inc.** Your second stop is close by. Go on up Bullion to 12th, turn left and proceed two blocks downhill. Just like that you've reached what someone has described as "the finest small museum to be seen anywhere." It shares a structure with the public library. Admission is free although donations are encouraged. Upon entering, seek a "Visitor's Self-Guided Tour" folder and turn left into the Daulton Room.

The first thing that caught my eye there was an 1853 price list. It indicated you could get a shave and a haircut for $1.50, a lawyer's word of counsel for $10, a pail of water for 10 cents. These prices, while quite high for the times, were probably typical for a gold rush town. A number of displays are loosely tied together by quotations from letters. The letters were written by Horace Snow from the original county seat community of Agua Fria in 1852–54 to a boyhood friend named Charlie back in Cambridge, Massachusetts. These letters to Charlie give quite a personal spin on how life was when gold mining was all the rage. You can see the press used by Mariposa's first (1854) newspaper, *The Chronicle*. See, also, how the Bull Creek School and Ben Hur Ranch were outfitted in the 1850s.

When you've absorbed as much as you want indoors, go outdoors and walk around the building counter-clockwise, noting the evolution of gold mining equipment from gold pan to stamp mill. Take note, also, on the north side of the museum, of the gifts of Native Californians to the History Center: two *u'macha'* (cedar bark dwellings) and one *tca-pu-ya* (sweathouse).

There's much more here than I've even hinted. Nevertheless, I'm suggesting, third and finally, a visit to the . . .

3. **California State Mining and Mineral Museum.** It is located on the Mariposa County Fairgrounds on Highway 49 1.8 miles south of the Highway 140/49 junction. The exhibit here has roots extending at least to 1865 when the California State Geological Society began a collection of gems, minerals, rocks and fossil specimens. From 1899 to 1983, the collection had the Ferry Building in San Francisco as its home. Its permanent siting in Mariposa was officially celebrated on September 5, 1987.

Children visiting the Museum will be particularly pleased to find objects on a counter with the unexpected instruction: Please touch. Folks of every age will like what lurks beyond the Mine Entrance. Deep in the 200-foot-long walk-through tunnel you find three exhibits dedicated to drilling, to blasting, and to timbering, mucking and tramming. You see a tram car loaded with ore. During actual mining operations, cars like these were moved to a main shaft and then lifted to the surface. I used my one-foot-long shoe to gauge the little railroad track. My finding: 18 inches. Sometimes it's handy to have a twelve-inch foot!

Emerging from the dimly lit shaft, you'll enter the mining wing. There, among other things, you'll see an Assay Office and a working scale model of a five-stamp quartz mill. One display reminds us that we're indebted to minerals for such things as aluminum cans, gold and silver jewelry (pretty obvious), but also gum, toothpaste, and cosmetics (to me, much less obvious). While you're here you can see, all in one place, the official California state gem (benitoite), mineral (gold), rock (serpentine) and fossil (*Smilodon californicus* or saber-toothed tiger). How's that for a bonanza?

Within the museum building is the Museum Shop, which has for sale a wide range of items appropriate to its setting.

Further Explorations

Can you give the general area a second day? If so, I recommend an easy hike down a stretch of the lower Merced River Canyon. You can see wildflowers in abundance, hear the sound of the rushing river, feel a gentle up-canyon breeze, get five miles worth of exercise! I'd give a day to cut a deal like that almost anytime, wouldn't you?

This hike is a walk. It's all along the right-of-way of the now defunct Yosemite Valley Railroad, and for the most part is nearly level. At a few points it's necessary to clamber over some old slides; nevertheless, this walk still bears my wife's seal of approval. (There are some up-hill hikes in this book that don't get that seal.) We hiked this canyon with another couple on the last day of March and liked it a lot. Many factors contributed: ideal temperature, river running fairly full, wildflowers blooming profusely and displaying such a pleasing variety of color and form. We identified California poppies, blue-pod lupine, elegant brodiaea, Ithuriel's spear, pretty face, plains wallflower, and white globe lily. With respect to shrubs, the western redbud was dressed its best.

We left our car at Railroad Flat and walked down-river for 2½ miles. There, where the North Fork enters the main river, we ate our lunch. Near our lunch site, we took particular note of North Fork Falls, actually a cascade of about 15 feet on the main river. So dangerous is this descent that river rafters are required to portage around it (as we noted in Chapter 19.) While the trail was by no means crowded, there were a number of other users. Some were on mountain bikes and were making a 20-mile roundtrip between Railroad Flat and Bagby. In a number of spots they had to push their bikes, and they even faced several short carries.

Two bits of advice and two of caution. Apply sun-screen and carry water. Keep a watchful eye out for poison oak—we saw plenty—and rattlesnakes—we saw none.

Access is by way of Highway 140 northeast from Mariposa. Taking the U.S. Forest Service Ranger Station in Mariposa as a starting point, drive up Highway 140 to Briceburg (12 miles, 20 minutes). At Briceburg, turn left and take the narrow one-lane bridge across the Merced River and ease down a dirt road 4.9 miles (but another 20 minutes). Now you're at Railroad Flat. Leave your car there and begin your walk down the old railroad right-of-way.

Best Time to Go

The best time to make the Merced River Canyon hike is early to mid spring. You want to go before it gets too hot, and when the wildflowers are blooming. Wildflowers aside, there are some days in the fall and even in the winter when this could make a nice outing. If walking on a hot summer day doesn't trouble you, you can relish the reward of a cooling dip in a pool in the North Fork.

As mentioned above, courthouse tours are available weekends from Easter to mid-October.

Mariposa Museum: Closed in January; open weekends 10:00 to 4:00 in February and March; open daily 10:00 to 4:30 from April through October; open weekends 10:00 to

4:00 in November and December.

California State Mining and Mineral Museum: Summer (May 1 to September 30): open daily (except Tuesdays, but including weekends and holidays) from 10:00 to 6:00; Winter (October 1 to April 30): open Wednesday through Sunday from 10:00 to 4:00. (Closed Mondays and Tuesdays).

Nuts 'n' Bolts

If you're coming up from Highway 99 at Merced, your distance and time to Mariposa will be 37 miles and 45 minutes.

If you want to go back toward Merced by an alternate route, you may choose Old Highway. It begins one-half mile north of the fairgrounds and rejoins Highway 140 at Catheys Valley. It's pretty slow going, but if it's wildflower season, and you're in no hurry, then I recommend it.

Key Contacts

Mariposa Museum and History Center
P. O. Box 606
Mariposa, CA 95338
209/966-2924

California State Mining & Mineral Museum
P.O. Box 1192
Mariposa, CA 95338
209/742-7625

Mariposa County Chamber of Commerce
P. O. Box 425
Mariposa, CA 95338
209/966-2456

CHAPTER 22

Fun by Some Dam Sites

Some dam trivia: (1) On National Forest land throughout the Sierra Nevada range, how many dams have been built? Answer: 467. (2) Of all the Sierra rivers, which one flows unblocked by any dam? Answer: the Cosumnes. Incidentally, authorities think the name Cosumnes (ko-sum-nes) is most likely of Miwok derivation, a piecing together of *kosum* meaning salmon and the suffix *umne* meaning tribe or people. I'm picturing a tribe taking many salmon from this river.

I'm not going to suggest that you seek out all 467 dams. No, I have only three dams in mind, along with their attendant rivers and reservoirs. All are located in eastern Madera County, situated to the east of Highway 99 south of Merced and north of Fresno. Here's your agenda for the day: **Friant Dam on the San Joaquin River making Millerton Lake; Hidden Dam on the Fresno River making Hensley Lake; and Buchanan Dam on the Chowchilla River making Eastman Lake.** I'm going to take up the three clusters north to south; however if you prefer to visit them south to north, feel free.

1. **Buchanan Dam** impounds waters of the relatively small and intermittent Chowchilla River. It was completed by the U.S. Army Corps of Engineers in 1975, mainly for flood control but also for irrigation, recreation, and fish and wildlife management. Recreation facilities were completed in 1979, and Eastman Lake was soon drawing an average of about 100,000 visitors a year. And then, boom! On June 20, 1989, hydrilla, a noxious water weed, was discovered in the lake. Fishing, boating and swimming were prohibited. And what do you suppose happened to the visitors? All but about 27,800 (in 1990) went somewhere

else or stayed home. This despite the fact that the area remained open for camping, picnicking and hiking. I'd advise you to call before making a trip.

The lake — officially H. V. Eastman — bears the name of a Chowchilla judge who was a driving force in getting this project going. When full, the lake contains 150,000 acre-feet of water, much of which is released for irrigation.

The dam — rockfill with impervious core — has a height of 205 feet and a length of 1,800 feet. It is named for a community which no longer exists. Back in 1873, however, Buchanan had a population of about 200, and most of its men were employed in the mining of copper ore. Some 50,000 tons of ore were taken from this vicinity prior to 1903. (You may find different — and erroneous — figures on a roadside monument).

The Corps of Engineers has installed boat ramps on both sides of the lake. The ramp on the west side is primarily for day-use visitors, while the one on the east primarily serves persons occupying camp sites. Speaking of camp sites, you have some choice here. The main campground is Codorniz with 62 sites, featuring hot water showers, flush toilets, a trailer dump station and even a public telephone — and, oh yes, a nightly fee (March through September). Further from the boat ramp is a more primitive 19-site campground called Wildcat. It has piped water, portable restrooms — and an appealing price: free.

2. **Hidden Dam,** about a half hour and a drive of 18.5 miles south from Buchanan Dam. Here the river in question is the Fresno. Like its neighbor to the north, Hidden Dam is also a Corps of Engineers project. It has less height, but much greater length than Buchanan: 163 feet by 5,730 feet. It was completed in 1975 at a cost of about $32.1 million, and is of the same type construction as Buchanan. Hensley Lake is smaller than Eastman, holding 90,000 acre-feet when full.

I suggest you begin your visit at Park Headquarters (at the north end of the dam). There you can see skeletal remains of a number of species of animals. When you leave Park Headquarters, drive below the dam and over to the south side of the lake where there's a vista point offering a grand view. Hensley offers the same range of recreational options as Eastman, actually more just now, being hydrilla-free. Boat ramps are located at

Hidden View campground (north side) and Buck Ridge Day Use Area (south side). Camping is a bit more limited here: 52 sites on a first come, first served basis.

3. **Friant Dam** and Millerton Lake on the San Joaquin River. (Incidentally, let Fresno County have credit for half of this lake; the county line dissects it.) Like Eastman and Hensley, Millerton Lake is a low-elevation lake, and multi-purpose: flood control, irrigation and recreation. It caters to both day-use people and campers. Held in place by a concrete dam, it's substantially larger than its neighbors to the north, with 43 miles of shoreline stretching some 16 miles up the San Joaquin River canyon. It's older, having been formed in 1944, and some would say too popular. Only about 20 miles from downtown Fresno, the lake sometimes attracts 25,000 people on a busy holiday weekend, and it draws an estimated 750,000 visitors a year.

Unlike the other two lakes, Millerton is a State Recreation Area under California's Department of Parks and Recreation. In the summer its family and group camp sites must be reserved through MISTIX (800/444-7275). Hours: 8:00 a.m. to 5:00 p.m. daily. You may charge your reservation to your American Express, Discover, VISA, or MasterCard.

Visiting all three lakes in a day poses no problems. Take a picnic lunch and enjoy it wherever hunger strikes.

Further Explorations

If you were to camp, you'd open up lots of options for yourself. For example, the eight-mile round-trip hike to the upper end of Eastman Lake (Raymond Bridge) can be a delight on a lovely spring day. On a day-trip basis, you have no time to indulge in such digressions.

Best Time To Go

Spring's the thing. Early April may embrace the peak of the wildflower season. Fall can be pleasant, but the water in the reservoirs may be greatly diminished.

Nuts 'n' Bolts

If you're touching all the bases north to south, Chowchilla is where you turn to the east off Highway 99 onto Avenue 26.

At a signed junction, take Road 29 out to Eastman, then after returning to the junction, take Road 603 (Daulton Road) to Hensley. To reach Millerton Lake will require the use of Roads 400, 406, 209, 145, and finally 206 into the community of Friant at the base of Friant Dam. All that entails some twists and turns, but with a detailed map of the area, the route is not difficult to follow. From Chowchilla out to Eastman is a run of about a half hour.

Key Contacts

U.S. Army Corps of Engineers
Eastman Lake
P. O. Box 67
Raymond, CA 93653
209/689-3255

U. S. Army Corps of Engineers
Hensley Lake
P. O. Box 85
Raymond, CA 93653
209/673-5151

Millerton Lake State Recreation Area
P. O. Box 205
Friant, CA 93626
209/822-2332

CHAPTER 23

Grover Hot Springs State Park

Did you know the State of California offers hot tubbing? Oh, yes! Its tub is of such a size, we'd better call it a pool. Approved for up to 50 people at a time, in the summer it's used by up to 400 people a day. This tub is two and a half feet deep, drained and cleaned every night, ready for service the next morning, and it is hot at 102 to 104 degrees!

Grover Hot Springs — named for an Alpine County family that used to own the meadow embracing the springs — has been in the state park system since 1958 and is located 3.7 miles west of Markleeville, out Hot Springs Road. That information helps a lot of folks very little. They need first to know: where's Markleeville? When they hear it's 32 miles south of Lake Tahoe, they generally nod with comprehension. Markleeville is the Alpine County seat. Even with that distinction, it would be a tough place to operate a theater or to get support for a professional ball team. That's because if you threw a party and the whole town came, you'd only have about 165 folks present!

Grover Hot Springs' elevation is 5,840 feet, which prompts me to remark that all the trips in this fourth section of the book have at least this in common: they take you upwards of 4,000 feet, and if you have problems with high altitudes, please be forewarned. This 519-acre park has 76 campsites. The night I car-camped there, at least 75 folks turned out for the ranger-led evening program. Junior Ranger programs for children aged 7 to 12 are offered most summer days. Temperatures in August typically range from a low of 45 to a high of 90 degrees.

Returning to the subject of pools, I should report that the "hot pool" is supplemented by a "cold pool." It's not really cold at about 80 degrees; however, when you enter it right after cooking at 102, believe me, it feels cold. At first I mistook it for snow melt, but then it felt very nice. This pool ranges from 2½ to 6 feet in depth and holds up to 25 people at a time. Changing rooms, restrooms and showers are right there on site; however, be prepared to pay an admission fee.

The park's uniqueness, of course, relates to the springs, but you can do other things besides soak. You can hike, fish, and, in the winter, go showshoeing and cross-country skiing. The park is open year-round, and there remains a place to camp (no showers available) even after the main campground has been shut down for the off-season. Since hours vary seasonally, call for current times. One thing that commends the park as a destination is that the routes to and from it are so scenic. In chapter 39 I tell of a double crossing of the Sierra via the two highest highway passes, Tioga and Sonora. On this trip you can conquer the third and fourth highest passes, Ebbetts at 8,730 feet and Carson at 8,573 feet.

Distance is not an issue here. From the Mother Lode town of Angels Camp to the park via Highway 4 is 88.7 miles; from Jackson to the park via Highway 88 is 88 miles. Both routes offer gorgeous lake views. Examples are **Lake Alpine** on Highway 4 and **Silver Lake** on Highway 88. Photos of either could easily grace a scenic wall calendar. Still, the two drives differ markedly. Highway 4, fine for quite a while, becomes narrow, steep and crooked, with lots of 20 to 30 m.p.h. stretches. You can enjoy it once, while your curiosity is being satisfied; as a commute, it would be a nightmare. Highway 88, on the other hand, offers excellent, full two-lane pavement along its length. You can sail over Kit Carson Pass at 50 m.p.h. if you wish. If you're going to do the loop, my recommendation is to go up Highway 4 and get its rigors behind you while you're fresh; save Highway 88 for a relatively relaxed drive home.

Imagine you're riding as a passenger in a car from the Valley to the higher reaches of the Sierra and you fall asleep. After awhile you wake up and, not having an altimeter, you wonder how high you have climbed so far. Simply check what species of pine tree you're driving by, and you should be able to estimate your elevation within one to two thousand feet. If you observe open-crowned grayish pines not very particular about growing straight up, you're amidst Digger pines (*Pinus sabiniana*) and you haven't climbed very high yet. Diggers are the lowest elevation pine, and you are likely to transition out of them somewhere in the two-to three-thousand-foot range. Suppose you awaken amidst ponderosa or western yellow pines (*Pinus ponderosa*), how high are you? If you're east of Sacramento or Stockton, you may see ponderosas below 3,000 feet, and you will probably be out of them before you reach 6,000. Further south, the range may run slightly higher. Stephen Arno in *Discovering Sierra Trees*[1] remarks on the ponderosa's ability to prosper on hot, arid sites, and he tells of a study which found this: "Four-year-olds averaged a foot in height but had sunk their roots five feet into the parched earth."

What if you wake up to sugar pines (*Pinus lambertiana*)? Most likely you're between 4,500 and 7,500 feet, and the trees are enjoying comparatively moist conditions. Arno writes: "Sugar pine is the tallest, largest, and by most accounts the most magnificent of all the world's more than 100 species of pines. Its great reddish- brown trunks and towering crowns, made up of long limbs that stand out at right angles, dominate millions of acres of mountain forest from western Oregon to Baja California." The cones average a foot in length, and dangle from branch tips like Christmas tree ornaments.

If you awaken to see stands of Jeffrey pines (*Pinus jeffreyi*), you're most likely in the 6,000 to 9,000-foot range. Arno acknowledges that folks sometimes confuse Jeffreys and ponderosas. "Each species bears its luxuriant 8- to 10-inch-long needles in bundles of three;" however, close examination reveals distinguishing features in cones and bark. *Discovering Sierra Trees* says: "This is the rugged pine most often seen clinging to stark granite domes and gleaming rock slopes overlooking the major Sierra canyons."

What if you're driving among western white pines (*Pinus monticola*)? Well, you may be about to run out of highway. In the Sierra, western whites are usually found between 7,500 and 10,500 feet, but in the Pacific Northwest they grow much lower. Only one more pine and we'll quit. Lodgepole pines

---

[1]Arno, Stephen. *Discovering Sierra Trees*. Yosemite Association, 1973. Used by permission.

(*Pinus contorta*), according to Arno, "occupy both slopes of the Sierra between about 6,500 and 10,500 feet . . . but (the species) often extends much lower along watercourses. For instance, it grows along the Merced River in Yosemite Valley at only 4,000 feet elevation. . . . Lodgepole is easily distinguished from other Sierra trees since it is the only one bearing needles in groups of two. The needles are also unusually stout and rather short . . . being about two inches in length."

Here's another idea: watch for the elevation signs posted along side the highway!

Further Explorations

If you have one or more extra days to roll into your travel package, you may wish to head on up to Lake Tahoe. I won't even start to list all you can do up "thataway."

If you want to reserve a camp site at Grover, phone MISTIX at 800/444-7275. Call 8:00 a.m. to 5:00 p.m. daily. There's a processing fee, and you can charge your reservation to your American Express, Discover, VISA or MasterCard.

Best Time to Go

True, you can get to Grover Hot Springs virtually year-round, but I believe most people would view this as a summer excursion. Clearly, crossing Ebbetts Pass is not for a winter outing; the road is closed. Early to mid-fall could offer you some glorious color.

Nuts 'n' Bolts

Angels Camp and Jackson, both on state Route 49, may be considered jumping off points. Just a little road map study can show you what you need to do to access those communities. If you're making the trip on a weekend, it might be a good thought to drive to or near one of these towns on a Friday evening, thus cutting down your Saturday driving time.

Key Contact

Grover Hot Springs State Park
P.O. Box 188
Markleeville, CA 96120
916/694-2248

Chapter 24

Triple Play:
Columbia Historic State Park
A Choice of Caverns
Calaveras Big Trees State Park

The first dish of this varied menu offers a glimpse of gold rush days, then you have an encounter with geologic time, and finally you meander through possibly the most marvelous sequoia grove in the world. Who could want a richer day than that?

Your jumping off place is Highway 49 just north of Sonora. If you come through Sonora, it's only 4.3 miles from the main intersection to the parking lot serving **Columbia State Historic Park.** What a rip-roarin' place Columbia must have been in those years following the discovery of gold on March 28, 1850. Around 1852 the town boasted four banks, three express companies, 26 produce stores, 30 saloons, seven bakeries, a printing office, theater, brewery, churches and lodges, schools, an amphitheater for bear and bull fights, four livery stables, and about 90 other businesses. Population soared to a high of about 6,000. The persistent miners wrested from area diggings some $87 million in gold, making Columbia one of the richest gold districts in the entire Sierra Nevada.

The community came into the state park system in 1945. The park has at the heart of its mission the maintenance of an atmosphere of 1850–1870. Try to organize your morning so as to arrive at the corner of Main and State at the William Cavalier Museum when the Columbia Gold Rush Slide Show begins (on the hour from 11:00 to 3:00). That will give you a good introduction to an era you've probably never encountered before. Note that fine live theater is offered here at Fallon House.

On to some caverns that are said to have a geologic history spanning 300 million years. It impresses me that bones of Native Americans found here are estimated to be 13,000 years old. Actually, you need to make a decision here between two sets of caverns which are about 7½ miles apart. Shall the choice be Moaning or Mercer? To go to both today would bust your time budget, so the thing to do is take your choice — you can't lose either way — and then come back to the area another time for the other. I truly like both caverns, much as I like peaches and apricots.

In your line of drive from Columbia to Calaveras Big Trees, **Moaning Cavern** comes up first. This cavern was first explored by gold miners in 1851 and is mostly one vast chamber. They say the Statue of Liberty could fit inside with some room to spare. There's a provision for rapelling to the bottom, but most tourists get thrills enough descending the long, steel, spiral stair-case. To access it from Columbia, you drive down Parrotts Ferry Road (E18), cross the New Melones Reservoir, and proceed to the signed turn-in to the cavern (8.9 miles). Now nine-tenths of a mile will bring you to where your cave tour starts.

If **Mercer Caverns** is your choice today, forget the just-mentioned nine-tenths mile and go 1.4 miles further on E18. Then turn right on Highway 4 for 3.3 miles. Now veer off to the left into Murphys and on out to Mercer Caverns (1.9 miles.)

The modern discovery of these caves is credited to Walter J. Mercer on September 1, 1885. Your guide will conduct you through some ten rooms, down multiple flights of stairs, for a total descent of 161 feet or 16 stories. Allow about 45 minutes for the tour, and enjoy the 55-degree cool. Bring a sweater. Both caves feature stalactites, stalagmites, columns, flowstone — though of these features Mercer is the more generously endowed. Both caverns charge for admission, and both offer spots where you can spread a picnic lunch.

Now off to another point of interest. Retrace your steps to Highway 4, turn left, proceed through Arnold, and, after

17.4 miles (from Murphys), park at the Visitor Center at Calaveras Big Trees State Park (admission fee). An informative 21-minute slide show begins on the hour from 10:00 to 4:00 daily during the summer. It is also available some additional weekends from 11:00 to 3:00.

Visit the small museum that is a part of the visitor center, then begin your third stroll of the day. With your just-purchased park brochure and North Grove trail guide in hand, set out on a one-mile loop trail which is nearly level. Identify the Empire State Tree with a base diameter of 33 feet. Pass through the walk-through tree. Budget about an hour for this richly rewarding stroll. I don't think you can get a superior sequoia encounter anywhere. Calaveras Big Trees have been a popular attraction since at least 1852, and in recent years the trees have attracted about 250,000 people annually.

Your trip home will take you back down Highway 4 to Angels Camp. Depending on your destination, I suggest that, one direction or the other, you drive county route E15, the 13.2 miles between Highway 4 and Highway 108. This will take you past Tulloch Reservoir, amidst some intriguing flat-topped mountains, and through a hamlet with the unlikely name of Copperopolis.

Further Explorations

Already I've mentioned the possibility of returning to see the cavern you chose to pass by on your first trip.

Then I also recommend going back to Calaveras Big Trees. On your second trip, pick up a South Grove trail guide and drive deep into the park to access the trailhead. Enjoy this delightful 3-mile hike among sequoias that are more dispersed than those in North Grove. Although you tour only a representative portion of the grove, you touch the largest sequoia grove north of the Kings River, containing nearly a thousand sequoias. A park ranger told me, "I like to have people experience the pristine nature of this special natural preserve. The only man-made objects we have here are a few signposts and two footbridges." After your hike, stop at the bridge across the Stanislaus. Swim (freeze) in the icy water. Then thaw out on the warm rocks defining the river's edges.

Best Time to Go

My own favorite time is early May because of the blooming dogwood in and around Calaveras Big Trees. Any time through the summer and deep into the fall should be fine.

Nuts 'n' Bolts

The turn-off to Columbia is from Highway 49 just north of Sonora. From a number of communities along Highway 99, your total distance for the day will be 200 miles, plus or minus. You'd better budget something like ten hours, say 8:00 a.m. to 6:00 p.m.

Key Contacts

Columbia State Historic Park
P. O. Box 151
Columbia, CA 95310
209/532-0150

Moaning Cavern
P. O. Box 78
Vallecito, CA 95251
209/736-2708

Mercer Caverns
P. O. Box 509
Murphys, CA 95247
209/728-2101

Calaveras Big Trees State Park
P. O. Box 120
Arnold, CA 95223
209/795-2334

Chapter 25

Highway 108 Country: Summit District of Stanislaus National Forest

One day I came zooming down by car from Sonora Pass to Sonora and on down into the San Joaquin Valley. I saw a lot of trees and formed the general impression that this was attractive mountain country. However, I didn't stop anywhere. I never saw a single subject enticing enough that I wanted to stop and take a picture.

There came another day when I had a chance to revisit this same area with a friend who knew what was tucked away here and there and how to reach it. On this latter day I stopped the car a number of times and took pictures I value still because they freshen my memory of . . . well, let me tell you of what. Valued memory number one is of **Pinecrest Lake** (5,620 feet). Check your odometer in downtown Sonora and roll east up Highway 108 for 29 miles. Watch for the fork in the road, and bear right for only a mile. Pinecrest Lake — what a beauty it is! You could spend a whole day right here, dividing your time among fishing, swimming, sunbathing, boating and hiking. There's a rewarding four-mile hike that circles the whole lake. My greatest single surprise on the hike was encountering several public telephones. I had been picturing myself way out in the mountains; nevertheless, here was Pacific Bell at my service!

Actually on this get-acquainted-with-the-area day, I suggest only a short stop at Pinecrest. That's because I'm eager for you to see three other places further along. Continue up Highway

108 from the Pinecrest junction (and the Summit Ranger Station), a distance of 3.6 miles and turn right on Herring Creek Road. Anticipate 4.5 miles of good, but not fast, paved road and 2.5 miles of dirt road.

That drive will take you to where you can walk the **Trail of the Gargoyles.** There's a South Rim Trail and a North Rim Trail. I suggest you take the latter and walk to where you get close-up views of some very unusual formations. Activate your imagination: what do you see? I saw, among other things, a bear and her three cubs. The trail guide, keyed to 11 numbered posts, will fill you in on the area's natural history. Budget roughly 2½ hours of time away from Highway 108.

Now, continuing east on 108, prepare to stop again 13 miles further up the road. A U.S. Forest Service sign says "Vista" and "Donnell." **Donnell Vista** (elevation 6,240 feet) offers off-road parking, restrooms, and the beginning of a ¼-mile trail leading down to an observation platform. The platform clings to the edge of the Stanislaus River Canyon and affords an especially fine view down into Donnell Reservoir, 1,320 feet below. The dam-created lake covers 425 acres and extends three miles up the canyon.

An interpretive panel says that in an average year 100 billion gallons of rain water and snow melt flow into this reservoir. The water is used five times to generate electric power. Then, says the panel, "In the valley it's used domestically, in industry, and to irrigate agricultural lands in the Oakdale–Manteca area." Donnell Vista offers you an extraordinary view.

Eastward and upward 7.7 miles. Now another USFS sign should come into view, and it should say "Geologic Site" and **Columns of the Giants.** Parking and restrooms are here, too. Take the trail which leads across the middle fork of the Stanislaus River and on to the base of a towering cliff. The cliff's face features columns 30 to 40 feet tall, estimated to be 150,000 years old. If you've visited Devil's Postpile National Monument you've already seen something similar to what stands before you here. The half mile roundtrip walk is virtually level and very easy. There's an interpretive display which will give you some of the geologic history.

At the Ranger Station just a mile from Pinecrest Lake you

can pick up a free and informative newspaper called *The Summit Passage,* published by the Three Forests Interpretive Association, as well as a fact-filled trail guide for the Shadow of the Miwok Prehistoric Trail, which is a quarter-miler just across the road from the Ranger Station.

Further Explorations

Plenty of possibilities are listed in *The Summit Passage,* available at Pinecrest Ranger Station.

Best Time to Go

May to October. However, please note that virtually all of the interpretive programs are limited to July and August. Some of the explanatory features that enhance the self-guided trails hibernate from about Labor Day to Memorial Day. The USFS takes them down and puts them away.

Nuts 'n' Bolts

You'd better allow fully two hours to get to Pinecrest, even from such nearer Valley points as Modesto and Merced. There are lots of camping and motel and food purchasing possibilities in the area.

Key Contact

Summit Ranger District
Star Route, Box 1295
Sonora, CA 95370
209/965-3434

CHAPTER 26

A Day in Yosemite Valley

A woman once asked Dr. Carl Sharsmith, "What would you do if you had only one day in Yosemite National Park?" "Madam," he replied, "I'd go sit by the Merced River and cry!" You will appreciate his response the more if you know that Dr. Sharsmith, Professor Emeritus of Botany at San Jose State University, has worked as a seasonal naturalist in Yosemite since 1930. In 1994, at age 91, he was still leading Field Seminars sponsored by the Yosemite Association.

His remark makes a valid point. Visitors having only a single day in the park will inevitably miss much that's wonderful. But far better than crying about the loss is relishing the gain. In a day you can "do" Yosemite Valley very well. After all, it's only about seven miles long and a mile wide. You can have a glorious and unforgettable visit in as little as three to five hours. If it were not so, Yosemite visitor counts wouldn't be surpassing four million a year!

As large as the state of Rhode Island, Yosemite National Park shelters 76 species of mammals, 230 species of birds and 1,400 species of flowering plants. It offers 450 miles of roads and 800 miles of hiking trails. In the next six chapters I'm going to describe how you can use up to six days happily exploring this vast treasure. But right now in this chapter I'm supposing you have only a single day and you've chosen to devote it to the Valley. What should you set out to see?

I suggest that you begin where the Park Service took Queen Elizabeth II of Great Britain to begin her visit to the Park on March 5, 1983: one of the most photographed vistas in the world, known as Tunnel View. You'll find it on the south flank of the western end of the valley at the eastern portal of a long highway tunnel. Yosemite's best known features are spread before you: Bridalveil Falls, El Capitan, Half Dome.

Before I identify the next stop on your Yosemite Valley tour, let me take you back to your point of entry to the Park. Regardless of which entrance station you passed through, I assume you were supplied with two handouts, one of which was a National Park Service combination map/brochure. I urge you to pull off into some safe parking and open the folder so that you see the enlarged map of the valley. Spend a few minutes reading everything to the right of the map and below. Later you can read the rest of the brochure, but right now learn about "Activities, Services, General Information" and "Protecting Yourself."

You will also have been handed a copy of the *Yosemite Guide*. Take a few minutes to browse through it with particular attention to the ranger-led activities scheduled for the day. You may wish to depart from my proposals because of something you've read in the *Guide*. The National Park Service has printed information available in Spanish, Japanese, German and French. If it would help you, or if foreign visitors are traveling with you, ask for the appropriate literature at the entrance station.

Returning now to Tunnel View, imprint the picture postcard scene on your mind. Linger a little. Then ease down the grade to the parking lot for 620-foot **Bridalveil Falls.** Take the short trail which leads toward the base of the falls. If the falls are raging and wind swirling, a dry towel would be a good thing to have along. Late in the summer Bridalveil quits altogether.

Now drive slowly into the heart of the valley. Where it is clearly safe to park off the road, yield to impulses to stop for closer views or picture-taking. Certainly you must stop roughly opposite Yosemite Falls (2,425 feet from the top of the Upper Fall to the base of the Lower Fall—fifth highest in the world). You'll get a much more intimate view of the Lower Fall later in the day.

Perhaps the Yosemite Chapel, coming up on the right, will engage your eye and interest. Built in 1879, it is the oldest building still in use in the park. In addition to its use by local residents as a non-denominational facility, it is often sought out as a wedding site.

When you reach the intersection take the right turn which leads to Curry Village. If you are visiting just for the day, park your car in the day-use parking lot at Curry Village and move around on the free shuttle bus system. If you're visiting at a time of low attendance, you can park quite easily in **Yosemite Village.** Regardless of where you leave your car, seek out the Visitor Center in Yosemite Village. See the fine multi- projector slide show in the theater. It supplies an excellent overview of the whole park and enables you to gain a good impression of how it is at other seasons of the year. Look at the displays, or ask any questions you may have of the park service staff. Outside the Visitor Center take a short loop stroll through the reconstructed Miwok Indian village that portrays Native American life circa 1872.

While you're at Yosemite Village, you can buy groceries, have a sit-down meal, shop, purchase stamps, mail postcards, or watch the amazing variety of fellow visitors. And when you've had your fill of the village, take the shuttle bus or drive your car a short distance to the west, to the parking area in front of Lower Yosemite Falls. From the parking lot, a trail—almost a road and fine for wheelchairs—leads about a quarter of a mile to the Yosemite Creek bridge that directly confronts the spectacular 320-foot **Lower Yosemite Falls.**

My own most memorable visit to the base of the Falls took place at night during a full moon. Several members of our family were staying at Yosemite Lodge. With flashlights along, but barely used, we walked to the bridge. There we sat and marveled at the play of the moonlight on water and granite. Talk about "some enchanted evening!" If you can plan your Yosemite visit in conjunction with the full moon, I'd encourage you to do so. You'll make for yourself a cherished memory. If everything comes together exactly right—lots of water, full moon, no clouds, just the right vantage point—you may have the extra special treat of seeing a lunar rainbow. A friend calls it an "almost mystical experience" and says his best observations have been from the little clearing east of the parking area where John Muir once had a cabin. The full moons of April and May probably offer you the finest chances.

Again, moving westward you're likely to see a small crowd

facing 3,593-foot tall **El Capitan.** These folks are straining to observe the progress of climbers who are ascending the face of this granite mass. You may want to stop and watch, too.

One more short stop remains. As you draw opposite Bridalveil Falls, be alert for parking on your left, right beside the river. Walk to the river's edge. Admire El Capitan from this perspective, and, if the water's calm, look for a spot from which you can see it both right-side-up and upside-down (reflected in the river) at the same time.

If you must leave at this point, I suspect you will want to return again soon. When you do, let it be with the intention of taking some hikes. You must get out on some trails.

Further Explorations

As already indicated, other things to do will be detailed in the next six chapters. Beyond that you can get many good ideas from the *Yosemite Guide* and others who have visited Yosemite more frequently. Many excellent publications about the park can be purchased in the park or by writing the Yosemite Association (see below). The free publication *Yosemite Magazine* is a rich resource and includes some great pictures.

If you want an in-depth park experience, many fine ones are offered by the Yosemite Association. Write for a catalog. There's something for almost every interest. There are shorter or longer, easier or more challenging backpacking trips, and seminars devoted to such subjects as photography, painting, Native American history, botany, the park fauna, etc. Knowledgeable leaders shepherd each group. If you belong to the Association —a good idea in any case—you qualify for a discount.

Important caution: Unfortunately, there is in the park a disease-producing micro-organism called *Giardia lambia.* Although the water looks clean and inviting, *do not drink untreated water from streams, lakes or snow.*

Best Time to Go

I think the best time to spend a day in Yosemite Valley is in the spring, when the waterfalls are most active and thunder down the canyon walls. Every season, however, offers sufficient rewards, which explains why the park's so popular. The traffic and crowds on Memorial Day, Fourth of July and Labor Day weekends should be avoided.

Nuts 'n' Bolts

A few words about getting there: to Yosemite Village the drive from Oakdale, via Highway 120, is 96 miles; from Merced, via Highway 140, 81 miles; from Fresno, via Highway 41, 92 miles. These are all good roads, but remember there are mountainous, crooked stretches which slow you down and call for speeds closer to 30 than 60 miles per hour. Allow two hours-plus from your San Joaquin Valley starting point.

Key Contacts

Public Information Office (Hours: 8:00–4:30, M–F)
P.O. Box 577
Yosemite National Park, CA 95389
209/372-0265

Other phone numbers, all but one in area code 209:
Road and weather information: 372-0200
Campground reservations: 800/365-2267
Hotel reservations: 252-4848
Sightseeing tours: 372-1240
Ski conditions at Badger Pass: 373-1000

Yosemite Association
P.O. Box 230
El Portal, CA 95318
209/379-2646

CHAPTER 27

Tenaya Creek and
Snow Creek Falls

I'm eager for you to see some of the glories of this great park that require walking, so I cordially invite you to take an easy hike up **Tenaya Creek** as far as its dashing tributary, Snow Creek. Begin at the Curry Village day-use parking area. Board the free shuttle bus. Get off at Stop 17 from which a road (no autos allowed) leads up to **Mirror Meadow,** formerly Mirror Lake, which geological change has filled with silt over the past 25 years. At the end of the road, look for the trail that continues up the left side of Tenaya Creek. Follow that nearly level trail for 1.6 miles beyond Mirror Meadow. There you cross Tenaya Creek on a substantial bridge. Once across, you can and should return to the Mirror Meadow Road on the horse trail that travels the eastern side of Tenaya Creek.

But don't return yet. If you've packed a sack lunch, here would be a good place to eat it. And, if it's spring, you may wish to walk on up the east side of Tenaya Creek for another several hundred yards. It's worth the effort in the spring because it offers what I regard as one of the most satisfying sights in the park: **Snow Creek Falls,** with its segmented descent. Four major sections of varying heights plummet very pleasingly down the western side of Tenaya Creek Canyon. I keep going back because it's one of my favorite falls in the park, but like many other spring water flows, it usually disappears by the end of June.

I must now add this word of caution: don't attempt to go further up Tenaya Creek. It offers difficult and dangerous terrain. The search and rescue people have too much to do already. Don't make them go looking for you!

Some pluses: the beautifully clear water of Tenaya Creek —named for Chief Tenaya (or Teneiya), the last chief of the valley-dwelling Ahwahnechee Indians—dances and sings as it prepares to merge with the Merced River not far downstream. You walk very close to it much of the time, and the world seems fresh again, unspoiled. Usually about the time April turns to May, dogwood blossoms decorate the landscape in a most attractive way. Deer often appear to the delight of many walkers on this route. And a special perspective on Half Dome (8,842 feet above sea level at its top, and about 4,700 feet above its base where you're walking) is guaranteed. Let your eye travel slowly up that vast, forbidding surface.

Well, so much for my reasons for hiking up Tenaya Creek. It's really a pretty modest challenge when you consider the levelness of this lovely loop. And it can serve, too, as a good tune-up for some heavier hiking later on.

Further Explorations

See previous chapter—and those to follow.

Here's another possibility. Perhaps you're planning an overnight in the park. Do check into the possibility of attending a ranger-led campfire program.

Best Time to Go

Answer: when the dogwood's blooming, when the upcountry snow's melting, when the streams are running full and swift. Translate that to calendar time, and it reads April/May. However, don't feel restricted to these months. You can take this trail earlier in the spring and later in the fall than any of the other Yosemite hikes I describe in this book. Remember, it's a fairly level walk and only about five miles in length. You could do it comfortably in a couple of hours.

Nuts 'n' Bolts

If you're doing this from the San Joaquin Valley as a day hike, you need to budget two hours-plus of driving time each way.

Key Contacts

See Chapter 26.

CHAPTER 28

Taft Point and the Fissures

This is the shortest and easiest of the six Yosemite hikes I'm recommending. To call it a hike is perhaps to overstate the case; "walk" may be better. From the trailhead to **Taft Point** is only 1.1 mile and most of that is gently downhill. Of course, it's gently uphill coming back. Twenty-five minutes down, 35 back should be realistic time allowances for many walkers. But don't go for speed; enjoy yourself.

The stroll through the woods, especially when the route is decorated with wildflowers, could alone warrant the trip. Then roughly 100 to 200 yards short of Taft Point five huge cracks or slits punctuate the canyon rim. You can—cautiously, I urge— peer down hundreds of feet to a canyon which opens southward from the main Merced River canyon (Yosemite Valley). The fissure nearest Taft Point has two large rocks lodged in it, and provides, I think, your most interesting fissure view.

Taft Point itself and its truly awesome view warrants the trip as well. Fortunately, with a protective railing right at the edge, you can walk to the brink with confidence. But if you've brought children, guard them as if their lives are at stake. Even with the railing, the drop-off commands your attention. After all, there are not many places where you can look straight down about 3,500 feet. Yosemite Valley looks a little like an architect's rendering of some new project. The trees, the river, the cars, the people—all seem rendered in miniature.

There's nothing miniature, however, about what lies across the valley: massive El Capitan directly opposite, Yosemite Falls a little to the east, and then further east, right in the geographical center of Yosemite National Park, Mt. Hoffmann, topping out at 10,850 feet. Unpack your sack lunch and sit a spell. Savor and soak in the sights.

By the way, two hours should be a reasonable time budget for all I have so far described. But now let's assume you want more exercise in your day. **Variation No. 1:** The same trailhead that serves Taft Point also serves **Sentinel Dome** (8,122 feet). It, too, is only 1.1 mile away. Perhaps the principal difference here is that it's up going and down coming back. It is a hike, but a relatively easy one.

If you choose to take it, I'd encourage you to do so before going to Taft Point. Although watching lightning strike across the Sierra may be a riveting sight, Sentinel Dome would be a poor choice of location if an afternoon thunder storm were to blow up.

Sentinel Dome is a great granite eminence. It offers gratifying vistas all around. And it is home to one of the most photographed trees in the world. I doubt that anyone knows how many calendars this gnarled, wind-blown Jeffrey pine has graced. Even now in death—having died in 1976—its weather-worn branches will call you to stop, admire, and think thoughts about tenacity in the face of adversity. It's an easy 1.1 mile back to your trailhead and car. And then you can set out afresh for Taft Point.

Let's suppose now that you know right up front that you want to take a substantial hike. Simply commit to **Variation No. 2.**

By this variation you go initially to Sentinel Dome, but instead of returning directly to the trailhead and then setting out for Taft Point (Variation No. 1), you begin to descend the northeast flank of Sentinel Dome until you intersect the Pohono Trail. Then it's a major descent until you bottom out at **Sentinel Creek.** On the way down, you'll have the most fabulous views of Yosemite Falls available anywhere. You can see the white water all the way down—including that intermediate stretch between the Upper and Lower Falls. Also, there are wonderful framing possibilities for the careful photographer. After crossing Sentinel Creek, many of those feet you've so effortlessly descended you now have to buy back. You've got to haul your body up a serious elevation gain until you merge with the trail running out to Taft Point. Then, it's easy going.

I confess I'm often attracted to loop hikes, having a certain reluctance about retracing my steps. There's no question that this is a fine loop, but equally, no question that it is a real hike. So, if you're short on either time or stamina, stay with the easier options. In any case, don't miss Taft Point and the fissures.

Further Explorations

Beyond the trailhead, readily accessible by road, are two points Yosemite visitors should certainly see, namely Washburn Point and Glacier Point. The former offers a particularly rewarding view of Vernal and Nevada Falls and the mountains to the east. Glacier Point offers a similar view and a blacktopped trail that enables the disabled to go right to the brink and thrill to this aerial view of Yosemite Valley as well as Half Dome and Tenaya Creek Canyon. There are restrooms, fast food, and a gift shop at Glacier Point.

If you're heading south, towards Fresno, and still have time, stop at the Yosemite Pioneer History Center. Note the covered bridge here and the lovely Victorian-style Wawona Hotel. *Wawona*, by the way, is the word the local Indians used to refer to the giant sequoias. You may wish to go on out to the largest grove of sequoias in the park, the Mariposa Grove, only six miles south of the hotel.

Best Time to Go

You won't have access to Taft Point until the Glacier Point Road opens, typically around Memorial Day weekend. Usually you can go deep into the fall. If you're wanting a showy volume of water in Yosemite Falls, then the earlier in the summer you go, the better. Toward the end of a dry summer Yosemite Creek can be almost completely devoid of water.

Nuts 'n' Bolts

With a Yosemite map in hand, it's no trick at all to identify the main route between Yosemite Valley and the southern points of Wawona, Oakhurst and Fresno (Highway 41). The Glacier Point Road intersects Highway 41 at a junction called

Chinquapin. Check your odometer here, and drive northeast 13.8 miles to reach the trailhead.

Key Contacts

See Chapter 26, the first of our seven chapters on Yosemite.

CHAPTER 29

The Panorama Trail

When you hike Yosemite's **Panorama Trail** you get the equivalent of three hits in one time at bat. You get intimate views —and some spray—from three of the park's most renowned falls: Illilouette, Nevada and Vernal.

The hike begins at Glacier Point (elevation 7,214 feet) and ends at Happy Isles (4,035 feet). You may know Yosemite well enough to see a problem with that. You finish walking about 3,200 feet below and about 8¼ miles away from where you started. Retracing your steps would be a distinctly unhappy prospect, so do one of two things: enlist someone to drop you off at Glacier Point first thing in the morning and pick you up at Curry Village late in the afternoon, or go up from the valley on the morning bus.

You begin by walking from the upper parking lot at Glacier Point straight out to the Merced River Canyon rim. There you will see a sign for the Panorama Trail, followed by the names of the three falls you'll visit and the distances. It's only two miles to Illilouette, and after a very short ascent at the beginning it's all downhill.

Be alert, as the trail seems about ready to level off, for a very short spur trail to the left. Walk down it and be rewarded by the full top-to-bottom view of 370-foot high **Illilouette Falls.** Press on a short distance to where a bridge spans beautiful Illilouette Creek. Assuming a 10:00 departure, your watch will read eleven-something. I urge you to pretend it's lunchtime and eat. Take advantage of an ideal place to enjoy a meal and be refreshed for your only significant uphill stretch of the day.

From the creek the trail ascends, not steeply but steadily.

You'll find yourself climbing without let-up for fully three-quarters of an hour, making your way well above a sheer granite wall which rises almost vertically above the Merced River. Particularly as you near the top of your climb, you'll be rewarded by the extraordinary views that give the trail its name.

My dictionary defines "panorama" as "an unobstructed view over a wide area." Left to right, you look back to Glacier Point. You peer down into the eastern end of Yosemite Valley, and your eyes take in the plunges of both Upper and Lower Yosemite Falls. Straight across the canyon, the unfamiliar back side of Half Dome looms. To your right you have Nevada Falls, and well beyond it, a horizon dotted with the peaks of the Sierra crest.

For roughly a mile the trail is nearly level, then it switchbacks down to the top of 594-foot **Nevada Falls.** A bridge spans the Merced River just above the massive cascade. Cross the bridge and make your way down to the guardrail. There, over the protective railing, peer straight down the distance of two football fields. Station yourself for a few minutes. See the whitewater tumble away toward Emerald Pool immediately above Vernal Falls, and let your eyes travel up to Glacier Point. Note Liberty Cap looming over you to the right, and at its base observe the tiny people laboring up and down the ever twisting trail—the Mist Trail upon which you will soon be descending yourself.

To pick up the Mist Trail, head up-stream for about two-tenths mile, then veer left for the abrupt, almost stair-steep descent. Take your time because this patch is a real knee-pounder. Proceed to the top of 317-foot **Vernal Falls,** where you can rest and take pictures.

Departing the ledge at the top of Vernal Falls, walk up the sloping granite south from the stream. You'll come to stairs which will facilitate your descent to the portion of the trail that gives rise to its name. Especially in early June with the river really rampaging, you can expect a full-blown shower bath. If you wear glasses, you'll want to turn on the windshield wipers; if you've been hot, now you'll be cool—not to mention wet. Soon you'll find yourself at the bridge below Vernal and here you'll mingle with many walkers who have ventured the short distance up from the valley floor. Figure about 20 more minutes down to Happy Isles, where you can board the free shuttle bus for Curry Village. It will likely be in the 4:00 to 5:00 range when you reach Curry.

Let me enter here my word of caution. Although this hike is largely downhill, it becomes long and wearing as the afternoon wanes. Be sure you have very comfortable shoes; trim your toe nails; maybe put some lamb's wool in the toes of your shoes. You'll want an adequate supply of drinking water. If you are below an average fitness level, the smart thing would be to listen to someone tell you about this hike. Some people in pretty fair condition regularly endure pain in their calves for several days following this descent. They aren't accustomed to stepping down roughly 4,000 feet in five or six hours.

When I wrote a newspaper article about this hike, I took as my title, "The Grandest Walk in the West?" There are western walks I haven't taken yet, and this may not be the grandest, but then again, possibly it is. Certainly it's a great one; a more scenic eight miles would be hard to imagine.

Further Explorations

If you're staying in the park, consider a ranger-led camp-fire program or consult your *Yosemite Guide*.

Best Time to Go

June. Any earlier and the Glacier Point Road probably won't be open; much later and the volume of water in the falls will be greatly reduced — and remember, water is a lot of what this hike is about.

Nuts 'n' Bolts

Here are a few statistics that may prove helpful. Coming from Highway 99 at Merced, it's a distance of 68.7 miles to the Arch Rock entrance station (figure an hour and a half). Then from the entrance station to Glacier Point, you've got another 32.7 miles (figure another hour of driving). Allow 2½-plus hours from most San Joaquin Valley points.

Key Contacts

See Chapter 26.

CHAPTER 30

Tenaya Lake and the Tuolumne Grove

How about exploring some parts of Yosemite to the east of the Valley and higher up? Enjoy a gorgeous lake and some awesome giant sequoias.

Let's begin with **Tenaya Lake,** which I regard as one of the most scenically-sited lakes in the high Sierra. Drive to the east end of the lake and park in the commodious parking area with restrooms right at hand. You'll notice initially the expansive, sandy beach. Now, do you begin your 3.1-mile walk around this 8,163-foot elevation lake clockwise or counter-clockwise? I tilt toward counter-clockwise, which will have the effect of saving the best for last. It will also have you safely facing oncoming traffic as you stride out westward on the edge of Highway 120.

On your right you'll see Polly Dome speckled with rock climbers. Continue on to the west end of the Tenaya Lake. At some point, you must cross Tenaya Creek. You may have to wade, or perhaps you'll find some stones you can tiptoe across without losing balance. In a wet year early in the summer, the water can be thigh-high. Make your way past the last of the old (now closed) walk-in campground sites and proceed to skirt the south side of the lake. A good deal of the time you will walk amidst lodgepole pines and hemlocks, and the cross-lake views are marvelous. Although the trail is not level, it is more of a walk than a climb. Back at the east end of the lake, you may test your balance on a log which spans the stream feeding the lake, or you may have to wade again. If you're something of a polar bear, you may even want to go for a swim in the lake. There are picnic tables adjacent to the beach. If you began your hike around ten, now should be an ideal time to break out your lunch.

Ready for the adventure of the afternoon? Following Highway 120 west for about 31 miles, you'll see a good-sized parking area on your right in the vicinity of Crane Flat. Find the trail that leads to the **Tuolumne Grove.** Note that this trail was once a one-way paved road. Presently, however, driving is prohibited and you must walk. The good news is that it's only one mile and all downhill. The bad news is that it's uphill, a climb of 500 feet (think 50-story building), coming back to your car. This is one of three sequoia groves in the park. The others bear the names "Merced" (same size as this one, only 15 to 20 mature trees) and, near the park's south entrance, "Mariposa," the largest by a wide margin, but not easily included in today's itinerary.

When you reach the Tuolumne Grove, take the little road that branches to the right, and give yourself the rather singular experience of walking right through the middle of a long dead tree. Proceed another 100 to 200 yards and begin your stroll around a three-tenths mile nature trail, replete with interpretive plaques. Along with some standing giants, there's a fallen one which is perhaps the most arresting feature on the loop. A Yosemite Association trail guide states that the Fallen Giant is 230 feet tall and 17 feet in diameter at its base. It contains 13,600 cubic feet of wood in its trunk, whose decay is retarded by tannic acid in the wood.

Don't limit your attention to the big trees. Make the acquaintance also of the tallest of the pines, the sugar pine (*Pinus lambertiana*), incense cedar (*Calocedrus decurrens*), white fir (*Abies concolor*), dogwood (*Cornus nuttallii*), and alder (*Alnus rhombifolia*). When you complete the loop, step across the road and admire several of this grove's largest specimens, then begin your uphill trek back to your car.

Further Explorations
See all the other Yosemite chapters (26–32).

Best Time to Go
Full streams making for magnificent waterfalls are not an issue here. So almost any time is a good time — within the

bounds dictated by snow and road access. The Tioga Pass Road usually opens toward the end of May and closes with the first substantial snowfall in October or November.

Nuts 'n' Bolts

Come into Yosemite via whichever of the three western-facing entrance stations is handiest for you (Highways 41, 140, or 120). Make your way to Crane Flat and follow the road that heads toward Tuolumne Meadows. Crane Flat to Olmsted Point is 29.4 miles and should consume nearly an hour, assuming respect for the speed limit and an interest in your surroundings. From Olmsted Point you can see Tenaya Lake a short distance further east.

Key Contacts

See Chapter 26.

CHAPTER 31

May Lake and Mt. Hoffmann

You may wonder: why this interest in Yosemite's 10,850-foot Mt. Hoffmann? There are higher peaks in the park, such as Mt. Lyell at 13,114 feet and Mt. Dana at 13,053 feet. I'll give you four reasons for my recommendation.

1. For visitors coming from the San Joaquin Valley and other points west, **Mt. Hoffmann** is handiest. You don't have to drive quite so far or climb quite so high. Even so, I'd rate this outing the most physically demanding in this book. It's not the longest hike described in these pages, but this one has you hoisting your body up roughly 2,000 feet from a fairly high elevation start, and your body may not be fully adjusted to the altitude if you've just come from the floor of the Central Valley.

2. Mt. Hoffmann has a unique location: right at the geographical center of Yosemite National Park. There's nothing approaching its height in any direction for miles, so you have a totally unobstructed view in all directions. Especially pleasing is the great stretch of the Sierra crest you see to the east, and Half Dome and Sentinel Dome to the south. The sheer drop off the north face of Mt. Hoffmann is itself a memorable and perhaps scary sight, although the marmots that call the peak home apparently are unconcerned about the chance of a 1,200-foot fall.

3. The hike offers the opportunity of visiting one of the High Sierra Camps. You may not be familiar with these camps. With proper reservations you can go on foot or horseback around a six-day, 53-mile circuit, counterclockwise out of **Tuolumne Meadows,** with stays at Glen Aulin, May Lake, Sunrise, Merced Lake and Vogelsang. How comparatively easy it is! Prepared

meals, comfortable beds, little to carry — who could ask for more?

At May Lake you can preview one of these camps. Getting there is relatively easy. You park your car only 1.2 miles away. There is an excellent trail, only moderately uphill, right up to the 9,320-foot lake. Forgetting Mt. Hoffmann and spending a big chunk of the day at the lake may appeal to you. Swimming isn't allowed here, but fishing and relaxing are fine. The May Lake High Sierra Camp can sleep 36 people in a cluster of tent cabins. It has chairs for 40 at four tables in the dining hall. Since its occupancy rate borders on 100 percent, you need to seek reservations prior to December 1. (See "Key Contacts" for details).

4. The hike is beautiful. May Lake itself is a gem with Mt. Hoffmann rising sharply behind it. In the early stages of your climb, you have a succession of wonderful looks at the lake from above. At this elevation spring comes in July to August. I say that with assurance because I relished the colorful displays of "spring" wildflowers on the ninth of August. Moving from flora to fauna, you have an excellent chance of seeing deer and marmots. Resist feeding the marmots, who will be begging for handouts.

Lodgepole pines and hemlocks are the predominant conifers as you leave the lake, while the top third of the hike features treeless landscape. The abrupt drop off the summit's north face notwithstanding, there's a comfortable, nearly flat area up top. It's a good idea to get up top fairly early. Thunderstorms may intrude later in the day, and you don't want to be on a peak like this when the lightning's popping. Ample water, sun screen and dark glasses are necessities.

The mountain is named for a German civil engineer, Charles F. Hoffmann, who did topographical work around Mt. Whitney. There is written record of the climbing of Mt. Hoffmann as early as 1863. Let me comment about climbing time. People climb at different speeds. I spent about two hours and a half from car to summit, but my wife thinks I'm a fast hiker and it's not a point I choose to argue. The complete roundtrip is about six miles, and hiking times will vary.

Assuming you're not lingering at the lake, let me guide you up the mountainside. The trail from May Lake on up requires more time and better conditioning. If you have the time and energy, leave the main trail and walk to the left along the south edge of the lake. The trail is quite easy to follow. Soon it begins to ascend a small gap to the southwest. For awhile it stays near a two-inch black plastic pipe which goes up to a water source on the hillside. After toiling up quite steeply for perhaps a quarter of a mile, you will reach a lovely little meadow maybe 125 yards long. The trail skirts left, passes among some trees, and then works its way up a ridge to the hiker's right.

As you surmount this ridge, you may observe the trail meandering somewhat imprecisely through what amounts to a hairpin turn. Now you face a long, relatively straight trek up a ridge which keeps increasing in steepness. Looking ahead you'll see a large outcropping of rock. You may think it's the summit, your destination. Sorry to disappoint you; it's one of two or three false summits. Soon you'll reach a vast tree-free plain and see the trail bearing somewhat to the left toward a rocky eminence topped by a radio transmitter. That's your objective! The grade now diminishes somewhat, but you're still in "huff-puff" territory.

At the base of the final peak, you'll see that you have a hundred yards or so of steep, rocky terrain still to cover. There's no defined trail here, and you may need to use your hands at several points, but it's really negotiated quite easily. Presto! There you are at the top of the mount!

Lunch time, right? Before descending the mountain, you may wish to walk over to the east rim (one of the false summits) for a spectacular bird's eye view of May Lake. Rejoin the trail on which you came up and follow it back down. Don't experiment with any other route; you could quickly get yourself in trouble. When you reach May Lake, stop at the High Sierra Camp for a nice cool drink.

Further Explorations

If you wish to stay a night or two at the May Lake High Sierra Camp, follow the procedure outlined under "Key Contacts." If you want to stay at Porcupine Creek campground, know that it is classified as primitive, meaning no flush toilets. You need to bring your own water, or treat the water that's there before drinking it. The sites are available on a first come, first served basis.

Best Time to Go

Assuming you want the High Sierra Camp to be open, your months to go are July and August.

Nuts 'n' Bolts

From Crane Flat to the left turn off Highway 120 toward May Lake is a distance of 27.6 miles. Figure about 45 minutes driving time. From the junction to the parking lot/trailhead is 1.8 miles. In order to get a reasonably early start on the climb, it would be good to overnight somewhere in or near the park. The Porcupine Flat campground would be the handiest of all.

Your 1.2 mile hike from the parking lot to May Lake is likely to require about 35 minutes.

Key Contacts

See Chapter 26.

If you are seeking High Sierra Camp reservations at May Lake or elsewhere, here's the process you need to follow: write Yosemite Concession Services Corp., Reservations Office, 5410 E. Home Ave., Fresno, CA 93727. Request a brochure entitled High Sierra Vacations. Fill out the official lottery form (one panel of the brochure). Mail it in between October 15 and November 30. Let me quote for you the three most critical of the 12 Application Guidelines.

1. High Sierra Camp Lottery Application Forms for the following summer are accepted by Yosemite Reservations from October 15 to November 30. Lottery applications received before or after these dates are not accepted.

2. Applications will only be accepted when on the official High Sierra Camp Lottery Application.

9. The lottery is held in mid-December. Applicants will be notified by the end of March as to their standing in the lottery.

For answers to any questions about procedures, call the High Sierra Desk at 209/454-2002. If no answer, call 209/252-4848.

CHAPTER 32

Indian Ridge and Its Natural Arch

If you were to ask 100 visitors to Yosemite in a random way, "Where is the natural arch?" nearly all would give you a blank stare and ask back, "What natural arch?" If the arch's existence is a secret, it's one I don't want to keep. I have enjoyed my visits to this unique feature very much, and I'd like for you to relish it, too. It does require a hike, but one I rate as moderate. If you're willing to stride right along, walking from trailhead to arch should occupy only about an hour and a half.

The arch is located between Highway 120 (Tioga Pass Road) and North Dome, and I would call it the crown of **Indian Ridge.** The arch itself is roughly six feet high and 28 feet long. You can climb around to the back side and see Half Dome through it. It's a spot you'll want to linger in. Assuming for the moment you're going no farther from your car, you may wish to break out lunch here.

The formula for getting to the arch may be written: down, across and up. From the Porcupine Creek trailhead on the Tioga Pass Rd., 25.6 miles east of the highway junction at Crane Flat, you descend seven-tenths mile along the remnants of a road to a now-extinct campground. The next section of the hike is relatively level and it's easy to make good time. Trail junctions are well marked for North Dome as a possible final destination. At roughly the one-hour mark into the hike, you are toiling up the west side of Indian Ridge and will encounter a sign indicating a side trail that you must take. Then you scramble rather steeply uphill for three-tenths mile. As you get close to the base of the arch, skirt it to the right and climb it from the back side.

Your return hike is easy until you cross Porcupine Creek seven-tenths mile from the trailhead. That last stretch may be breathtaking in the most literal sense of the word.

Further Explorations

I've tried to keep my hike recommendations somewhat on the easy to moderate side, with nothing too taxing (although some might raise questions about Mt. Hoffmann). Going on out to **North Dome** may be more than you care to do. Let me tell you about my experience, then you decide.

After coming down the three-tenths mile from the natural arch, I descended to North Dome in about 55 minutes. Some of the descent was fairly steep, which I certainly noticed coming back. As I approached the dome itself, there was a final gentle ascent, and I soon found the bench mark certifying the elevation as 7,532 feet. Magnificent views rewarded my efforts. As I faced Glacier Point across the valley, I had 8,842-foot Half Dome close-by on my left, and slightly to my right dramatic views of Yosemite Valley stretching away to the west. Even a simple peanut butter sandwich tastes great in such a setting as this.

The peculiar thing about North Dome is how it can look so lofty from the valley floor and require so much uphill climbing back to your car when you leave its virtually bald pate. I'm offering you fair warning. When I left the dome, I faced the hardest, hottest section of the hike. I climbed constantly for about an hour and a quarter, most of that time without benefit of shade. Total round-trip distance: about 9.6 miles. I was away from my car for five hours and 45 minutes. Many would probably have wanted a slower pace. This is an excellent and rewarding hike, but—no question about it—it is a hike!

I want you to be aware of another hike option using this same trailhead. It features visits to **Yosemite Point** and the top of **Upper Yosemite Falls.** The principal problem you have to overcome is this: you must find someone to drop you off up top (Tioga Pass Road) and pick you up at the Chevron Station down in the Valley (Yosemite Village). Your walking distance will be about ten miles and your time allowance should be somewhere around 5½ hours.

This hike has several distinct pluses in addition to being mostly downhill. Yosemite Point offers fantastic views up, down and across Yosemite Valley. From the trailhead to the Point took me about two hours. Supposing a ten o'clock beginning to your hike, the Point will be an ideal place to stop for lunch. The top of Upper Yosemite Falls provides dramatic views, too, and maybe just a little scariness if you don't like heights. The steep, crooked descent to the Valley floor is rich in additional scenic vantage points. Figure about two hours for the descent.

Finally, with regard to Yosemite hikes, I feel I should say a word about climbing **Half Dome.** The National Park Service rates this hike "extremely strenuous" and well it should. From the Valley floor it requires an elevation gain of about 4,800 feet and a roundtrip distance of about 16½ miles. From Glacier Point the distance expands to 19.8 miles, but you don't have quite so much elevation to gain. One August 17th a friend and I made the trip from Glacier Point. We had left Merced at 3:30 a.m. and were on the trail at 6:00 a.m. and we got off the trail at five minutes to six p.m.

Despite its difficulty, the hike is very popular. In my opinion, the easiest trip would have you leaving from Glacier Point and, after doing the Dome, descending to the Valley by the John Muir Trail. For that you'll need someone to drop you off at Glacier Point in the morning and pick you up in Yosemite Valley at the end of the day. Even the easiest way is a strenuous hike.

Best Time to Go

July, August, September. You should be able to go in June or October. It is always advisable to check with Park Headquarters before starting a difficult hike.

Nuts 'n' Bolts

Make your way to Crane Flat (T-type highway junction between Yosemite Valley and the Big Oak Flat entrance station.) There check your odometer and proceed 25.6 miles eastward toward Tioga Pass. At that point, a sign saying "Porcupine Creek" should come into view. There's plenty of off-pavement parking, except possibly on weekends. Locate the trailhead and hit the trail. Here, again, the usual cautions: carry ample water and food; protect yourself from the sun; dark glasses recommended. Camera and binoculars are urged as well. The post-hike drive back to Highway 99 at Merced is nearly 120 miles, for which a time allocation of two hours and 45 minutes should be realistic.

Take note: access to Half Dome is not from the trailhead just described. For Half Dome you begin from the Valley at Happy Isles (beyond Curry Village) or from Glacier Point.

Finally, as a point of emphasis, let me repeat that while I consider the natural arch a moderate hike, the other options are physically challenging. If you are not in good health and condition, leave these demanding treks to others.

Key Contact

See Chapter 26. This concludes our treatment of trips in Yosemite National Park.

CHAPTER 33

Fresno Dome · Nelder Grove · Corlieu Falls

Do you like a day marked by variety? Hikes on the short side? If so, this tour's for you! Pick Oakhurst (Junction of Highways 41 & 49) as your point of departure. All your driving from that point and back to it should not exceed 45 miles. Your walking will amount to about three miles in three hikes.

Off we go to our first objective: **Fresno Dome,** a magnificent head of granite that tops out at a mostly bald 7,540 feet. If you saw a 1991 movie titled *The Giant of Thunder Mountain,* you've seen Fresno Dome already. It had a supporting role in the film, much of which was shot on location at Kelty Meadow. Locate the meadow on your map and stop if you like.

From the Highway 41/49 junction in Oakhurst, it's 2.4 miles up to the Ranger Station, where you may wish to pick up some literature. From the Ranger Station continue on Highway 41 for another 1.7 miles. Turn right on Sky Ranch Road. Proceed 8.3 winding, uphill miles and then bear left on a road signed for Kelty Meadow and Fresno Dome. After 3.1 miles, you'll have another left turn. Now only 4.5 miles should separate you from the Fresno Dome trailhead, which you will find at the back (east) side of the dome after parking in the clearly marked parking area. Oakhurst to the trailhead should take under an hour.

On foot from this point, you have only seven-tenths mile to cover to reach the top. Half of that distance is fairly level; the other half is up a mostly moderate incline. Altogether, 30 to 40 minutes should see you to the summit. One caution: part way up the northwest side of the dome, at a large Jeffrey Pine

159

(three feet in diameter and with a missing crown), a trail for rock climbers goes straight ahead. Don't go straight; turn sharply to your left and continue on the trail uphill.

The top of the dome is spacious and affords fine views in all directions. Unfortunately, the air is often so polluted that you can't see as far as the valley floor. Under happier circumstances you could see clear to the Diablo Range. I sometimes say to people, "If the air over the valley was water, you'd refrain from swimming in it, wouldn't you? And yet many of us breathe it day after day." The scenery close by is lovely. Much of the way you walk among red fir (with the lovely scientific name of *Abies magnifica*), Jeffrey and sugar pines. Quaking aspen (again a suggestive scientific name: *Populus tremuloides*) add a delightful, trembling accent to the tiny meadow adjacent to the parking area, and the fluttering golden leaves are quite a sight in late October.

If you want to camp close by, the Fresno Dome Campground is only 2.8 miles down the dirt road from the trailhead and offers 12 sites on a first come, first served basis.

If you're ready now for the second scenic treat of the day, do this: retrace your route. A few miles down Sky Ranch Road watch for the signed right turn to **Nelder Grove.** Proceed to Nelder Creek and a small parking area on the east side of the road. There you'll see the well-signed beginning of the Shadow of the Giants Trail. The trail forms a loop, up one side of the creek and back the other side, about a mile roundtrip. Make the loop clockwise and don't rush. The route is replete with very interesting interpretive signs, from which I learned or was reminded that . . .

• Giant sequoias (*Sequoiadendron giganteum*) once had a vast range. Today they're limited to 70 small groves, perhaps 60,000 mature trees on the Sierra's western slope from Placer County to Tulare County. If all the trees were gathered in one grove, the area they cover would be a little less than half the surface of Lake Tahoe.

• Sequoia roots rarely exceed eight feet in depth, but they do spread out, sometimes covering between two and three acres.

• One tree along the trail is credited with these statistics: 272 feet tall, 71 feet base circumference, 170,000 board feet of timber, enough to build 17 five-bedroom houses. However, the wood is so brittle it has long since been rejected for construction purposes. (You say you know of redwood lumber? That's the coastal redwood, *Sequoia sempervirens*).

• For a tree so large, the seeds are surprisingly small. It takes 3,000 to add up to one ounce! A tree may produce 60 million seeds in its lifetime. Perhaps three or four will result in trees living 100 years or more.

Nelder Grove was partially logged in the 1880s. It contains sugar pine, cedar and white fir intermixed with the sequoias. The grove—named for John A. Nelder, a '49er who lived in the area after failing as a miner—was acquired by the U.S. Forest Service in 1928. The Shadow of the Giants trail was constructed in 1965 and designated a National Recreation Trail in 1978.

One more super scenic spot still to see: **Corlieu Falls.** Drive back down Sky Ranch Road to Highway 41 (roughly nine miles), turn right and proceed 3.3 miles. On your right you'll see an "Elevation 4,000" sign. Cover another hundred yards and then park on a very broad shoulder. Spy out a trailhead at the east end of the parking area and follow the trail down toward Lewis Creek at the bottom of the canyon. A sign will soon indicate one-tenth of a mile to Corlieu Falls.

The Falls are named for Charles Clifford Corlieu (1861–1929), who is buried just a short way off the trail. If you're alert, you should spot the sign that marks his grave. Corlieu hailed from Missouri and engaged in both logging and ranching in the Auberry area, east of Fresno, for quite some time. When one of his daughters took up residence in Sugar Pine, upstream from the falls, Corlieu built a cabin above the falls in order to be near her. A piece of Forest Service literature says, "In his last years of peaceful retirement, Corlieu wrote a book of verse speaking of his love for God, his fellow man, and the glories of nature. The surroundings which inspired him can be enjoyed today along this trail."

I suggest you go to the foot of the most downstream cascade. That will require going more than one-tenth of a mile and markedly more climbing to come back up to the road, but what you see warrants the extra effort. The bottom cascade, with a turn like a bent elbow, is beautiful, while the main fall, just a bit back upstream, is poetry in motion. Water finds several routes of descent before entering a lovely pool, and attractive foliage wraps the whole scene. Corlieu ranks very high on my list of truly beautiful falls. I always enjoy going back.

Now it's only 5.1 miles back to the Oakhurst Ranger Station, and just a little further to Oakhurst itself.

Further Explorations

If you're spending a second day in the vicinity, consider driving the Sierra Vista Scenic Byway (Chapter 34).

Best Time to Go

It's largely a matter of the snow having melted so that you can drive to the Fresno Dome trailhead, which might not happen until June. Access should continue through October. While almost any time within this period should be fine, I'd say a day in June would be great for Corlieu, while a day in September or October might, by a slight edge, be better for Fresno Dome and Nelder Grove.

Nuts 'n' Bolts

If you don't live in Oakhurst, your first task is to get there. How you do that will depend on where you do live. If you live north of Merced, I would recommend going up Highway 120 to Mariposa and then south on Highway 49 to Oakhurst. If you live south of Madera, simply drive up Highway 41. Folks in Chowchilla/Madera and those coming over Pacheco Pass and through Los Banos should exit Highway 99 at Madera (Cleveland Ave.) and use Highway 45 to access Highway 41. Your road map should make all this perfectly clear.

Key Contact

Mariposa Ranger District (of Sierra National Forest)
41969 Highway 41
Oakhurst, CA 93644
209/683-4665

CHAPTER 34

Sierra Vista Scenic Byway

Before we meet the **Sierra Vista Scenic Byway** I'd like to introduce you to "Scenic Byways" in general. In 1989 the Forest Education Foundation released a brochure which listed the first 53 drives in the U.S. to bear this designation, all of which traverse National Forests. Among the original byways—more are being added as time goes by—three were in California: (1) 58 miles of the Carson Pass Highway (Highway 88), (2) 33 miles along the Smith River just south of the Oregon border (Highway 199), and (3) the one out of North Fork which I'll describe in a moment. Of the three, the only one which feels like a true byway to me is Sierra Vista. It meanders well off the beaten track and, unlike the other two, it is not a main line between points A and B.

The large horseshoe-shaped route approaches a hundred miles in length, requires the commitment of a day, supplies a fine overview of a major portion of the San Joaquin River drainage, and visits some highly unusual features. It takes you out Minarets Road to an elevation of over 7,000 feet and eases you back down to Bass Lake over Beasore Road. When you set out, stock up with a good supply of gasoline and a hearty lunch. Look forward to a minimum of seven stops.

1. Before you begin the actual byway, visit the **Minarets District Ranger Station** at North Fork and pick up the official byway brochure.

2. Ask at the Ranger Station about the **geographical center of California.** It's just a few miles out of North Fork, and a service club has been planning to build something showy to mark the spot.

3. **Redinger Overlook,** 7.1 miles from the Ranger Station. Here you're high on a hill peering down into the San Joaquin River Canyon. Your view features a lovely lake impounded by a dam.

4. **Mile High Vista,** 20.7 miles from Redinger Overlook. Noon should by now be near, and with picnic tables here and picture postcard views in several directions, bring out the food! The immediate view is down into Mammoth Pool, a reservoir created in 1959 when Southern California Edison Company built a 330-foot-high dam here. Lifting your eyes and looking more to the east, enjoy a stretch of Sierra crest, with peaks such as Mt. Ritter reaching skyward more than 13,000 feet. An interpretive panel identifies some granite eminences to the north as the "Eagle Beaks" (not Eagle Peaks). One of these aptly named peaks in particular is so strikingly realistic that I doubt a commissioned sculptor could improve on the likeness.

Rested and ready to go, proceed another 19.5 miles to . . .

5. **Arch Rock.** It will be on your right. The signing is modest, so don't blink. Park and walk diagonally downhill for about 30 yards. The arch's top is quite level. If you have confidence in your balance, you can walk across it. It spans very little really, but is sufficiently extraordinary to make your stop here rewarding. Another 5.6 miles will bring you to the junction with Beasore Road. Here you turn left and may think of yourself as headed homeward. However, it's along here that you confront the road's poorest surface. Some of it appeared to have been oiled once upon a time. Still there are dusty patches and some at least mildly rough surface, so slow down, and look forward to seeing, after 9.7 miles . . .

6. **Globe Rock.** The rock is on your left and can be seen from the road, but I advise walking back to it, an easy stroll of about 50 yards. I found this glacial erractic (a rock dropped when the ice carrying it melted) reminiscent of the large sphere which held a prominent position at the 1964 World's Fair in New York City. Drive another 1.1 mile and you'll be back on a good two-lane paved road.

7. **Meadow Vista.** This is my name for a sequence of gorgeous mountain meadows, awash in summer with a wonderful display of wildflowers. The green grass is a pleasant

change from the summer browns of lower elevations. Cows may be contentedly grazing in some of the meadows. Choose any meadow you like, and stop and savor it awhile; then continue down Beasore Road to Bass Lake, a very popular summer resort with waterskiing, swimming, and fishing as major activities. Pines Village, on the lake, offers gas, food, lodging, and various shops. Today, however, you may want to hurry right on to Oakhurst, where the main drag—Highway 41—could be somebody's idea of "fast food heaven."

Further Explorations

Note that 8.8 miles after Globe Rock you reach Cold Springs Summit (elevation 7,308) where you can enlarge your loop. By driving quite a stretch of dirt road you can see such rewarding sights as Fresno Dome and the Nelder Grove of Giant Sequoias. I recommend visiting these places but on another day. (Chapter 33.)

Best Time to Go

The route is not plowed, so you must go after snow melt. June to October is the time frame.

Nuts 'n' Bolts

Some distance east of Fresno and Madera, Highways 41 and 145 intersect. From that point, continue up Highway 41 in the direction of Oakhurst 8.9 miles, then turn right on Road 200. Another 17.8 miles will take you to stop number one: the U.S. Forest Service Ranger Station at North Fork.

Key Contact

Minarets Ranger District Office
P. O. Box 10
North Fork, CA 93643
209/877-2218

CHAPTER **35**

Huntington Lake and Environs

On the radio the weather forecasters were saying: "Expected high today in the Fresno/Clovis area, 105 degrees." Dressing for breakfast, I was putting on a tee shirt, long-sleeved thermal underwear, a sweat shirt and a down jacket. I welcomed every layer. You guessed correctly; I was not in Fresno/Clovis, but in a U. S. Forest Service campground south of **Huntington Lake,** roughly 75 miles east of Fresno, at an elevation of around 8,000 feet. It's cooler up there, certainly, and the coolness may be one of the attractions. In fact, there are so many recreational possibilities in this area that I could say here what might have been said about several other areas: "Too much to do!" Well, not really, but it takes some sorting out. I will sketch a favorite scenario to help you.

Let me assume that this area is largely unfamiliar to you. I will outline a day plan which will have two merits. It will be an interesting and rewarding day in its own right, and it will enable you to become aware of other things to do if you stay over one or more days or if you return to the area in the future. I recommend it heartily, even if you delete the two hikes and make it strictly an auto loop drive.

Drive up Highway 168 to the community of **Shaver Lake.** Seek out the U. S. Forest Service Ranger Station (which may be in a new location by the time you read this). Wherever you find it, it's precisely the place to go to pick up, as a minimum, sheets on two National Recreation Trails: Rancheria Falls and Black Point. If it's a weekend in July or August, I urge you to inquire about the Forest Service's Guided Nature Walks and Campfire Programs. On a week day, consider getting and following directions to the powerhouse and trout hatchery at Big Creek. Free 1½-hour tours are offered at 10:00 and 1:00 by Southern California Edison Company between June 15th and Labor Day. If you're staying over and like to hike, secure the four-page handout, *Suggested Day Hikes*, on the Pineridge Ranger District of Sierra National Forest. I'll have more to say about one of the suggestions later.

For now, set your sights on **Rancheria Falls.** A few miles above the village of Shaver Lake, note—but don't take—the road leading to Big Creek. At that point set your trip odometer to zero, and continue 16 miles on Highway 168 to a signed right turn. Now you have a drive of 1.2 miles uphill on an unpaved road to reach the trailhead.

The trail's only a mile long. Virtually all of that is a gradual ascent of 360 feet, bringing you to an elevation of 8,120 feet— and the bottom of the 150-foot falls! Because of the high elevation, snow can linger in these parts, as I found out one Memorial Day when snow covered the trail intermittently over one-third of the distance. In a heavy snow year, you might not have a completely snow-free trail until well into June. I think an hour and a quarter is a suitable amount of time to budget for the roundtrip hike.

Once back down to Highway 168, you have only six-tenths of a mile to go to reach the **Eastwood Visitor Center.** You may want to inquire about a USFS Picnic Area for lunch. From the Eastwood Visitor Center, and facing Huntington Lake, proceed to the right around the lake's east side. In six miles you'll reach the dam. Descend one mile more, and identify a well-signed junction bidding you to turn right onto a dirt road to reach **Black Point,** a second National Recreation Trail.

Go up this road 4.7 miles (and past two signed forks) to reach the trailhead. The trail is unremittingly up for its entire length of six-tenths mile. Your elevation gain will be 471 feet, topping out at 8,111, and near the top the ascent is severe— about a 20 percent grade. Enjoy a few deep breaths at each of the signs along the route that identify the flora you're seeing: white fir, chinquapin, bracken fern, white thorn ceanothus, gooseberry, sierra juniper, green leaf manzanita, and Jeffrey pine. Black Point offers a marvelous view of Huntington Lake (close by) and Shaver Lake (some miles away). I found an hour an adequate time allowance for this hike, but many may want a slower ascent.

Back in your car, begin to retrace your route. In a short distance you'll come to a sign saying **Mushroom Rock Vista.** Go for it. It's only three-tenths mile from the junction to the parking area; then you have an easy stroll of 200 to 300 yards to a large boulder which has a top of greater diameter than the stem. That's about as much as it has in common with mushrooms, but it's enough to support the name. There's a good view from here, too.

A forewarning on the dirt road: mostly it's fairly smooth, and you can hold 25 m.p.h. over much of it; however, there are four water diversion bars in the road for which you'd better slow way down. They are not signed and you'll need to watch the road carefully to anticipate them. Back at the black-topped road, the thing to do is turn right (downhill). Before you is a highly scenic 10-mile twisting route through the hamlet of Big Creek and back to Highway 168, only a few miles east of the village of Shaver Lake. So there's a rich day for you.

Further Explorations

In this locale, you can fish, boat, water ski, backpack, drive off-road vehicles, and so on, but there are three possibilities I want to identify specifically.

1. **A hike for the hardy.** Destination: **Lower and Upper Twin Lakes.** As to distance, it's six miles roundtrip. As to elevation, we're looking at surmounting 9,149-foot Potter Pass. The trailhead is 4.7 miles east of the Eastwood Visitor Center out the Kaiser Pass Road. I car camped at the Badger Flat campground the night before I took this hike, so that I was well positioned for an early morning start. On the trail at 6:45, I was at Potter Pass at 7:30, and at Lower Twin Lake at 8:10. Was I rewarded! At the time of my arrival, with no stir of air, the reflections in the lake were stunning.

It takes only about seven minutes to go on to Upper Twin Lake and more spectacular views. Usually I'm conservative in taking pictures; here I became an instant liberal. Click, click, click. I can't recall a time that I've burned more film in so few minutes. Here, too, the reflections were sharply etched; I've never seen any more perfect. Add a wonderful display of "spring" wildflowers in mid-August, a magnificent fir forest — nature's Christmas tree factory — and picturesque sierra junipers standing tall with white clouds dotting a blue sky above. Linger awhile and enjoy. My counsel is to spare yourself the time and effort entailed in climbing on up to George Lake, but the challenge is there for you if you want it.

2. **Florence Lake** (elevation 7,328) and **Edison Lake** (7,643) and **Mono Hot Springs** (6,500). If you pore over a map of the area, these features will attract your attention as they did mine. So I went out to see them. You may wish to do so, too, but before you go, let me ask you to weigh several observations.

On the plus side, you'll certainly see some magnificent mountain scenery while moving continuously on a blacktopped road. But . . . there's a price to be paid in miles and time. From Eastwood Visitor Center out to Florence, out to Edison and back to the Visitor Center cost me 60 miles and about four hours of actual driving time (with a few picture stops included). It's beautiful country, no question about that; but the road is narrow and crooked and gives rise to this question: how much time do you want to spend behind the wheel? My own personal tilt is to say that on a single day trip from the San Joaquin Valley, Florence and Edison require a burdensome amount of driving. If you're spending a night or two in the area, then a different assessment may be in order.

3. **Stump Springs Road / Sample Meadow / Kaiser Pass Road Loop.** This loop may one day be designated a Scenic Byway, similar to the one described in Chapter 34. Let me talk you around it, with Shaver Lake our place of beginning. Drive east on Highway 168. A short distance after leaving Shaver Lake, turn left where you see the sign "Big Creek 7." Continue out Stump Springs Road (USFS Route 5) and expect a lot of curves and reduced speed. About two miles beyond Big Creek the road becomes very good: smooth pavement, mostly two lanes, straight enough that you can hold 30-35 miles an hour much of the time. The pavement abruptly ceases at 27.2 miles, and

there remain 13.5 miles before you tee into the Kaiser Pass Road at a point 12.3 miles beyond the Eastwood Visitor Center. The 13.5 mile stretch is relatively slow going.

Going out along the south flank of the San Joaquin River canyon at elevations ranging from 5,000 to 5,600 feet, you have lovely cross-canyon views to the north. The Eagle Beaks are especially prominent. At one point the vista to the east, including Mounts Ritter and Banner, is especially attractive. If you wish to put a hike in your day, you can access the Twin Lakes from a trailhead a mile south of the Sample Meadow campground. This is an easier access than the one I mentioned earlier over Potter Pass.

Once on Kaiser Pass Road, you'll soon drive over the pass itself (9,184 feet). When you get back to the Big Creek junction above Shaver Lake, you will have completed a loop of 69.4 miles. If you eat lunch but don't hike to Twin Lakes, then 3½ hours should be a reasonable time allowance for the loop.

Some Cheers for "Development"

Whatever options you exercise, you may want to think a thank-you to Southern California Edison Company. It (and predecessor companies) are responsible for the existence of the area's four main reservoirs: Shaver (135,283 acre-foot capacity), Huntington (89,000), Florence (64,000), and (officially) Lake Thomas A. Edison (125,000).

Lake Edison was dedicated on October 19, 1954, simultaneously celebrating the 75th anniversary of the invention of the incandescent lamp on Oct. 21, 1879. The reservoir is created by Vermilion Dam on Mono Creek. Florence Lake is on the South Fork of the San Joaquin River. When you look up its considerable length, the most prominent peak you see is 11,013-foot Mt. Shinn, named for Charles Howard Shinn, Forest Supervisor of Sierra National Forest from 1905 to 1911.

Though these lakes cater heavily to recreation these days, they were brought into being primarily for the purpose of generating electricity. A series of tunnels and penstocks channels the water through a total of nine hydro-electric plants with a total capacity of 1,000 megawatts (1 megawatt equals 1,000 kilowatts). Other lakes in the system are Mammoth Pool and Redinger.

A Southern California Edison brochure recounts a bit of interesting history: "In 1911, the initial development of the Big Creek–San Joaquin Hydroelectric Project began. The first problem was how to get men and materials into the heart of the High Sierra. So a railroad was built to Big Creek—The San Joaquin and Eastern (SJ&E). With 1,100 curves, it was often referred to as the 'Slow, Jerky and Expensive.' It was a 56-mile line from a point 18 miles north of Fresno to the site of Big Creek Powerhouse Number One. The line was built in an unbelievably short 157 days. . . ." Rail service ended in 1933.

Best Time to Go

If you want to take the hikes, give the snow time to melt. The drive itself could be very pleasant as early as April/May and it could be lovely, too, say in October with some fall color in the area. For the area in general July/August would be prime time.

Nuts 'n' Bolts

Mostly it's a matter of gaining elevation, and you begin that process on Highway 168 out of Fresno/Clovis. If you live in Madera or farther north, cut across Highway 145 (following signing for Millerton Lake and Friant Dam). If you're coming down Highway 99, use the Cleveland Ave. exit at Madera. A drive of about 37.2 miles should bring you to the point of intersection with Highway 168. Turn left. Keep on the signed route.

Key Contact

Shaver Lake Ranger Station
P.O. Box 300
Shaver Lake, CA 93664
209/841-3311

CHAPTER **36**

Kings Canyon

Why do they call it **Kings Canyon**? Erwin G. Gudde's book *California Place Names* suggests that the canyon was named from the river, and the river was named by a party of Spanish explorers who reached it — much further down — on January 6, 1805. That was Three Kings Day or Epiphany. So they called the impressive stream *Rio de los Santos Reyes* (River of the Holy Kings). These are the same kings celebrated in the Christmas song "We Three Kings of Orient Are," whose journey is narrated in Matthew 2:1-12 of the *Bible*.

Let's pile on a couple more dates. Sequoia National Park ranks as the second oldest in the country, having been established by an act of Congress on September 25, 1890. Kings Canyon came along much later, in 1940. Today the two parks, embracing some 1,300 square miles, are administratively one. That is not to say that one day will suffice to see them. I believe you'll want a minimum of two days. You could put the days back to back, or make two separate trips. I'll describe a first day here for Kings Canyon, and then in the next chapter I'll propose a separate itinerary for Sequoia.

My advice is to drive up Highway 180 from the Fresno area, enter Kings Canyon National Park (there will be an admission fee), turn left and find yourself fairly soon at the **Grant Grove Visitor Center.** Here you can read the *Sequoia Bark* given you when you entered, find out what's going on, ask questions, and see a fine slide show for an excellent introduction to the park.

The next thing to do is to drive down into Grant Grove itself and walk the short loop trail on which you'll see the third largest tree in the world, "General Grant." This Giant Sequoia has been designated "the nation's Christmas Tree." On the second Sunday in December the Sanger Chamber of Commerce offers a special non-denominational worship service here. The tree stands 267 feet tall. The trunk weighs about 1,250 tons. The circumference at the base is 107½ feet, the diameter of the largest branch 4½ feet. General Grant's age is between 1800 and 2000 years.

Now, having had a wonderfully rewarding short walk, look forward to a highly scenic 30-mile drive down into Cedar Grove and the very heart of Kings Canyon. Highway 180 descends with many a twist until it parallels the river. By all means proceed further east; the road continues six miles beyond Cedar Grove. About halfway along on your right, park and take the short walk to **Roaring River Falls.** Of modest height, the falls have great vigor and beauty, whizzing down a granite water slide.

Shortly before road's end you may get out of your car and look up at **Grand Sentinel** towering over you about a mile to an ultimate elevation of 8,504 feet. In the event you're in the mood for a hike, you can take to your feet at Road's End, go up one side of the river to where Bubbs Creek enters, cross a bridge, and return on the south side of the river. Later you'll cross a second bridge to get back to your car.

Whether you plan to secure a campsite, seek out motel-type accomodations, or drive clear home, it's probably time to call it a day.

Further Explorations

If you're simply doing a day trip, I'd say stay with the program as outlined. If you want to ponder other possibilities, you might write ahead for literature. The National Park Service offers many enticing ranger-led activities and programs at a variety of venues.

If you would like to get in on a park-related educational experience of perhaps two or more days duration, inquire about the natural history field seminars sponsored by the Sequoia Natural History Association. Membership in the SNHA is available to all interested persons. Write SNHA, Ash Mountain,

Box 10, Three Rivers, CA 93271.

I should add for the benefit of cave aficionados that down in Kings Canyon but outside the National Park proper, you may visit **Boyden Cavern.** Guided 45-minute tours—cave temperature 55 degrees F.—are available daily from 10:00 to 5:00 from June through September, and from 11:00 to 4:00 during the months of May and October. For information phone 209/736-2708. There is an admission charge.

Best Time to Go

If you can visit before the summer season, then go while the water is most abundant in May and early June. On the way up the South Fork of the Kings River, well before Cedar Grove, there's a beautiful falls named Grizzly. Cedar Grove is usually closed from about November 1 to May 1.

Nuts 'n' Bolts

The distance from Fresno to Grant Grove via Highway 180 is 55 miles. So an hour and a half should be an adequate time budget to reach the Grant Grove Visitor Center. Perhaps the main feature of the trip is elevation gain—roughly 5,000 feet!

There are National Park Service campgrounds in both the Grant Grove and Cedar Grove areas. In the former you'll find Azalea, Canyon View, Crystal Springs and Sunset; in the latter, Sheep Creek, Sentinel, and Moraine. All are on a first come, first served basis. Azalea is the only one open all year. Sequoia National Forest provides some additional campsites close to the park. For details call the Hume Lake Ranger District office at 209/338-2251.

If you have company who would benefit from having park literature in Spanish, French or German, request it at one of the Visitor Centers.

Key Contact

Sequoia and Kings Canyon National Parks
Three Rivers, CA 93271
209/335-2856 (Grant Grove Visitor Center)

CHAPTER 37

Sequoia National Park

Now you're ready for **Sequoia National Park.** What a great day you have to look forward to! If you're coming up by way of Fresno, follow Highway 180 from the valley to and through the Big Stump Entrance Station. Turn right and head down the Generals Highway. Enjoy the scenery and set your sights on the **General Sherman tree.**

I don't know what it is about the biggest, or the oldest, or the tallest, but there's something magnetic. You want to make that extra effort to see it. Here you have the biggest of the Giant Sequoias, and it's virtually alongside the highway with its own parking lot. Its claim to surpassing General Grant (see the preceding chapter) rests largely on two statistics. The estimated weight of the trunk is 1,385 tons—134 tons more than General Grant. The volume of the trunk is estimated at 52,500 cubic feet—5,050 more than General Grant. Imagine what it has endured during nearly three millenia.

Drive on to **Giant Forest Village,** where there are a wide range of services. Then pick up the branch road that leads southeast and visit five wonderful locations. I'll put names to them.

1. **Auto Log.** If you like, you can drive your car right onto this long-fallen sequoia and go home with a picture.

2. **Moro Rock.** Here we have a massive granite 6,725-foot dome towering 4,000 feet above the Kaweah River, almost a toy stream in the canyon far below. From the parking area, it's a steep climb to the top. Over a distance of about ¼ mile, there are lots of steps to climb. If you are in shape, go assured that your expenditure of effort will be well rewarded. To the east

177

you'll look all the way to the Sierra crest and to the west far out into the San Joaquin Valley.

Back at your car, continue eastward. You'll soon come to . . .

3. **Tunnel Log.** You can't miss it. The road passes right through a long-fallen sequoia. You need to be sure that your vehicle can make do with less than eight feet of vertical clearance. If it can't, use the alternate route around the left end of the log. Continue on to road's end at . . .

4. **Crescent Meadow.** John Muir christened this green-carpeted opening in the forest the "gem of the Sierra." What a beauty it is, especially at the height of the wildflower blossoming season in late July and early August. Many species adorn the meadow. On one trip I saw probably the finest display of Sierra shooting stars (*Dodechantheon jeffreyi*) I've encountered anywhere.

5. **Tharp's Log.** Requires a bit of a hike, not very long, not particularly strenuous, but a hike nonetheless. If you go, you'll see where one Hale D. Tharp resided during the summers of 1861–1890. His home was a large, fairly hollow, fallen sequoia that he closed at the bottom end with roughcut boards and fitted out with a rock fireplace.

Further Explorations

I doubt that you can tuck these extras into a single day. Still, I want to make you aware of two options so fine that you may wish to stay over or come back.

1. The hike to **Tokopah Falls** from the upper reaches of the Lodgepole campground. The falls are not perpendicular, like some of the classic ones in Yosemite. I'd call them a cascade and credit them with great beauty. In season the wildflowers along the way are wonderful. The vertical granite wall on the south side of the stream is itself an awesome sight. Called The Watchtower, it soars over you some 1,600 feet.

The stream here is the Marble Fork of the Kaweah River. A piece of park literature says: "In a distance of 15 air-miles the Marble Fork drops 9,000 vertical feet—nearly two miles! The river that flows through Lodgepole has one of the steepest gradients of any river in the United States."

2. **Crystal Cave.** Here I think I can help you best by simply

quoting from *Sequoia Bark:* "A beautiful marble cavern featuring stalactites, stalagmites, and an underground stream . . . Crystal Cave is located nine miles from Giant Forest Village. Starting at the Village, drive two miles south on the Generals Highway, then seven miles to the cave on a side road (trailers, RVs, and busses not allowed). From the end of the cave road, walk ½ mile on a steep trail to the cave entrance. Allow one hour to get to the cave from Giant Forest."

Tours: Guided walking tours of Crystal Cave were not offered in 1993 because of the replacement of a bridge. In 1994 and after, tours will probably be offered between the hours of 10:00 and 3:00 daily during the height of the summer. **The Lodgepole Visitor Center** will have details. It's likely that you'll be required to get a ticket at the Visitor Center at least an hour and a half in advance of your tour. Tours last approximately 55 minutes. Take warm clothing because the cave temperature is 48 degrees.

Best Time to Go

May to November. I wouldn't discourage you from visiting anytime within that range; however, the wildflowers at Crescent Meadow are so magnificent that late July would be the ideal time.

Nuts 'n' Bolts

I touched on the trip up from Fresno in the chapter on Kings Canyon. Here let me forewarn you about your return to the valley. You descend possibly the steepest, crookedest stretch of blacktop anywhere in the bounds of this book. I can't recall anything that equals it. Don't fear or shun it; simply take it easy. Once pretty well down, you exit the park at Ash Mountain (Park Headquarters here), continue through the community of Three Rivers, and find yourself fairly soon in Visalia.

In the event you want overnight accommodations in Sequoia, let me list some possibilities. The park concessionaire, Sequoia Guest Services, has a variety of motel-type facilities at Giant Forest (also some cabins with and without bath). Winter lodging in Sequoia will not be available, beginning with the winter of 1994–95, until new facilities are in place.

The National Park Service maintains large campgrounds at Lodgepole (260 sites) and Dorst (218 sites). There are a couple of small campgrounds in the lower elevation part of the park (east of Three Rivers): Buckeye Flat (28 sites) and Potwisha (44 sites). Potwisha is open all year and some winter camping (likely in the snow) is possible at Lodgepole. Lodgepole operates on a reservation basis from mid-May until late September. Call MISTIX at 1-800-365-2267. All the others are first come, first served and are open only in summer.

Key Contacts

Sequoia National Park
Ash Mountain
Three Rivers, CA 93271
209/565-3134 for park information
209/565-3351 for 24-hour weather and road conditions recording

To contact the park concessionaire (room reservations, etc.), write:
Sequoia Guest Services Inc.
Sequoia National Park, CA 93262
209/565-3381 (call 8:00 a.m. to 5:00 p.m. daily)

CHAPTER 38

Mineral King

Mineral King is a relatively recent addition to Sequoia National Park. After escaping some 19th century development efforts and a 20th century Walt Disney offer, Mineral King entered the National Park system in 1978.

Earlier, prospectors had hoped to find significant deposits of gold and silver in the area. Although some of the precious metals were found, the quantities were consistently disappointing, and the southern Sierra never offered yields that compared favorably with findings in the Mother Lode well to the north. In the 1890s lumbermen cut significant numbers of giant sequoias, but the wood was never very satisfactory for construction, and the difficulty of removing it from the area was daunting. In 1906 the same earthquake that ravaged San Francisco caused avalanches that destroyed most of Mineral King's buildings. But the area's beauty was such that the community made a comeback, and today visitors cherish the valley's natural loveliness and summer coolness.

Access to the valley is gained by a 25-mile-long road (Route 276) which leaves Highway 198 about three miles east of **Three Rivers** (33 miles east of the Highway 198/Highway 63 junction —Mooney Blvd.—in Visalia). It's a slow 25 miles. One writer credits the road with 698 tight turns. I didn't independently verify the count, but as I drove the letters VCR took on fresh meaning: Very Crooked Road. A cabin owner told me it takes her and her husband an hour and half to negotiate the distance, "and, if we hurry, it takes an hour and half." My speed ranged from 15 to 25 m.p.h. virtually the whole way.

I talked with a resident of Three Rivers who had never

181

traveled to Mineral King because of the threat of car sickness. And I know some flat-land residents who would eschew this trip out of fear of tumbling into the East Fork of the Kaweah River. I'd say the road averages about a lane and a half in width. There's no center line, but generally two cars can pass with care. Three Rivers is at about 800 feet in elevation and Mineral King 7,500, so it's uphill all the way.

I chose to go on April 15, 1993. That was both a bad choice and a good choice. Bad because lingering snow forced a turn-around at the 17.6-mile mark, yet good for a number of other reasons. The wildflowers put on a show that ranks among the best I've ever seen. Both the range of species and the sheer quantity of flowers made the trip highly gratifying. I found myself stopping repeatedly to look at fiddleneck, poppies, brodiaea, Ithuriel's spear, lupine (two varieties), and Chinese lanterns, among others. If it is simply wildflower viewing that you're interested in, turn around at the **Kaweah River Oak Grove** bridge 6.7 miles up the road. The April-blooming flowers are fewer beyond this point.

On my visit, creeks that doubtless go dry by late spring skipped prettily down steep slopes. At 16.2 miles I was surprised to encounter two giant sequoias next to the road and right beside cascading Redwood Creek. I chose it for my lunch site. The temperature was ideal, and the song of the stream added melodic pleasure to what otherwise was stillness and silence.

Near the trees, which I judged to be about 12 feet in diameter, I spied a National Park Service exhibit that recalled August 20 and 21 of 1879. On the night of the 20th some 150 animal-drawn conveyances were clustered close to the creek awaiting the next morning's opening of the toll road to Mineral King.

My choice of day was good also because of the light traffic. With picture stops my drive in spanned an hour and half— and I saw one car! On a day-trip basis, you won't have much time for hiking at Mineral King. You might, however, fit in a quarter-mile stroll along the **Cold Springs Nature Trail.** It adjoins the East Fork of the Kaweah River and is shaded by cottonwoods and aspens. You may be treated to the sight of summer wildflowers and the sound of resident birds. Some eleven trails in the area lead out to magnificent high country.

But at that point we're entering another realm—that of the very fit.

By the way, Mineral King has two campgrounds: Atwell Mill with 23 sites and Cold Springs with 37.

Further Explorations

If you have an extra day, or want to return at a later date for another single day outing, then consider this option. From Three Rivers it's only 12.9 miles out to a Sequoia National Park campground on the South Fork of the Kaweah River. South Fork Drive is two lanes for 6.6 miles. It narrows but remains paved to the 9.7 mile mark. The rest of the way there's a dirt surface, but you can move right along. I covered the distance in 35 minutes.

I found this route lightly traveled. I met only one person, and she was on a bicycle. The wildflowers and redbud lent lovely color to the hillsides. At the campground two trailheads present themselves: the Ladybug Trail and the Garfield/Hockett Trail. Both lead to giant sequoia groves. Of the two, the second is clearly the longer, steeper, more physically demanding.

The easier Ladybug Trail will take you from 3,600 feet at South Fork Campground to 5,000 feet at Cedar Creek where the sequoias are. Be advised that this is not a large grove. I counted about a dozen mature trees. One way distance: three-tenths mile, round trip time allowance: 3 to 4 hours. Steve Sorensen, author of *Day Hiking Sequoia*, is enthusiastic about this trail: "Of all the foothill trails in the park, the Ladybug Trail is the most beautiful. In the summer it offers opportunities for swimming and fishing along the South Fork of the Kaweah. . . ." If there are younger children involved, he suggests going only to Ladybug Camp, a distance of 1¾ miles (elevation 4,400 feet). Steve's book describes 50 day-hikes available to you throughout Sequoia National Park. The South Fork Campground has 13 sites. The road in is not recommended for trailers or recreational vehicles. This is true also of the road to Mineral King.

Another possibility is to look into water-related recreation on Lake Kaweah between Three Rivers and Lemon Cove. This reservoir is a project of the Army Corps of Engineers.

Best Time to Go

If you're intent on getting in to Mineral King, better plan for June through September. If you're satisfied, as I was on April 15th, to enjoy the lower elevations, then spring or fall can work well for you.

Nuts 'n' Bolts

If you leave Highway 99 west of Visalia, at the Highway 198 interchange, figure about about 55 minutes (39 miles) to the start of the Mineral King road.

Key Contacts

Sequoia and Kings Canyon National Parks
Three Rivers, CA 93271
209/565-3134

Three Rivers Visitors' Information
41695 Sierra Dr.
Three Rivers, CA 93271
209/561-3212

CHAPTER 39

The Far Side: June Lake, Mono Lake and Bodie

According to the old song, the bear went over the mountain to see what he could see. I want to encourage you to go over the mountain—to cross the Sierra range—to see what *you* can see. There's a lot, not only *over* there, but *getting* there and getting back. I will lay it out for you; however, you for your part must budget two days at least, and one or two nights.

First, let's consider the going and the returning.

Going: I suggest you go through Yosemite National Park, topping out at Tioga Pass. At 9,945 feet, Tioga is the highest highway pass in the whole of the Sierra range. And what a dramatic descent it is from there to Highway 395 at **Lee Vining**. If you have some life-long "flatlanders" in your car, you may need to have them don blindfolds in order to keep their panic under control. I mean that it drops off alarmingly!

Make some vista stops, perhaps at Tioga and Ellery Lakes. Once well down the mountain side, pull off to the right for a look at the trout pond in front of the Lee Vining Ranger Station and relish the grand view of the sheer eastern face of the Sierra, rising to over 13,000 feet! Wildflowers may add to the attractive ambiance.

Returning: When heading for home, tackle the second highest Sierra highway crossing, **Sonora Pass** (9,624 feet). To reach this high point, drive north from Bridgeport 17.5 miles, turn left on Highway 108, and proceed 15.3 steep, crooked miles to the pass. On Highway 108 two things may merit short stops: one is Pickel Meadow, site of a U.S. Marine Corps Mountain

Warfare Training Center. Four large choppers were parked just to the right of the road when I last passed. And just over 9 miles from the Highway 395/108 junction a sign on your left should alert you to the existence of nearby Leavitt Falls. A walk of perhaps 250 yards will bring you to a precarious promontory from which you can peer far down into a constricted canyon. There Leavitt Creek makes its big leap on the way to joining the Walker River to the east.

Once at the summit, stop and read the plaque and reflect on the "good old days." When this route opened as a toll road in 1856, the roundtrip Sonora to Bridgeport—almost 200 miles—was rated a three week ordeal.

Let that suffice on the Sierra double-crossing. Please be introduced to several exceptionally interesting **features on the far side.**

1. **June Lake Loop.** At the Highway 395/120 West junction, turn right (toward Bishop) and travel a scant 4.3 miles. Here you turn right again, beginning now the 16.3 miles of state Route 158 which will bring you back out to Highway 395 a short distance east of June Lake. In that short distance, you'll come upon a lovely succession of four lakes. **Grant Lake** is surrounded by plenty of sage brush, but very few trees. **Silver Lake**'s surroundings are more scenic. You'll pass the small Rush Creek Hydro Plant of the Southern California Edison Company on your right.

Gull Lake is next. Like Silver Lake, it's scenically situated and popular for fishing; but campgrounds and other private land development are impacting the area. Finally you reach **June Lake**—both lake and town. At the east end of the lake, there's an area reserved for swimming, but one might need to be a walrus to relish it. Even in August, when you factor in the 7,650-foot elevation, that water has got to be cold!

Next, you may easily visit **Panum Crater.** If you choose to go, here's how to access it. From the Route 158/Hwy. 395 junction east of June Lake, go north on Hwy. 395 for 5.8 miles and turn right on Highway 120 East. Proceed 3.2 miles and then turn left on a dirt road. A drive of nine-tenths mile will take you to the crater parking area, from which you have a short uphill hike to the crater itself. Panum Crater features obsidian

from which the Paiutes fashioned arrowheads and other artifacts, and it offers excellent views of Mono Lake and the Sierra
crest to the west. The site is under the administration of Inyo
National Forest and bears the designation Mono Basin National
Forest Scenic Area.

2. **Mono Lake.** Continue eastward on Highway 120 1.7 miles
more. Turn left onto an unpaved road that drops you down to
the South Tufa Area Parking Lot. Distance: one mile. Look for
the Mark Twain Scenic Tufa Trail, maintained by the California State Department of Parks and Recreation. Twain visited
here in 1863, and interpretive signs along the trail quote a
number of his observations. The trail's about a mile in length.
Begin by following it to the shore of Mono Lake, one of the oldest
lakes in North America and currently covering about 40,000
acres. In 1941 the surface elevation of the lake was 6,417 feet
above sea level, but since Los Angeles' Department of Water
and Power (DWP) snared the water of four feeding streams the
lake has dropped in excess of 50 vertical feet.

This major drawdown has threatened to have catastrophic
environmental consequences. Islands in the lake serve as nesting
sites for many waterfowl, including 85% of this state's California gulls, who migrate between here and the Pacific Ocean.
When the water gets down to and below current levels, land
bridges to islands are opened, enabling mainland predators
access to the nesting areas. Not only so, but at the current
level, dust problems and increasing salinity threaten the ecosystem. In the view of The Mono Lake Committee (see below),
the lake really should be maintained at 6,386 feet, or about eleven
feet higher than the mid-1992 level.

Who will save the lake and the Mono basin ecosystem? The
story is much too long to recount here, but you see where my
sympathies lie. Drop in at the Information Center operated by
the Mono Lake Committee in the heart of Lee Vining; see the
slides; read the literature; become an advocate.

Meanwhile, back at the lake, there's one plus: while the
low water levels are unfortunate, they do allow you to walk
among these intriguing tufa formations. Interpretive materials
explain that "the strange-looking spires and knobs...were
formed when fresh-water springs under the lake interacted

with the alkaline lake water." The result? The unusual calcium-carbonate tufa structures. Mono Lake is "three times as salty and eighty times more alkaline than the ocean." The water has a slippery feel to it.

The trail takes you southeastward, following closely the contour of the lake. Fine vistas abound. In the spring and fall, you're almost certain to see some of the seventy species of migratory birds that visit the lake, lured here by the plentiful food supply of brine shrimp and brine flies. Fortunately, the flies—present in numbers that stagger the mind—take no interest in humans.

With your lakeside walk completed, drive to Lee Vining. I hope you still have time to visit the **Mono Basin Scenic Area Visitor Center.** Located just north of town, this $5 million facility was opened May 30, 1992, and is operated by the U.S. Forest Service. See the permanent photo exhibit and catch an interpretive audio-visual. Check to see if an evening program is scheduled.

Stay overnight in a local motel or area campground.

3. **Bodie.** From Lee Vining, drive north on Highway 395 about 19 miles. You'll have an excellent road and the early morning light will enhance the beauty of the landscape. At the well-signed junction, turn right towards Bodie. On the well-paved state highway proceed through sagebrush-covered hills for ten miles, followed by three miles of ROUGH AND SLOW. The abundant rocks protruding above the road surface make one very glad not to be a tire. But press on; even this trial will end and you will be at probably the finest ghost town in the state. Imagine this once being a thriving community of 10,000.

Actually there is now a sparse non-ghostly presence here in the form of three families employed by the California State Department of Parks and Recreation. The town is named (change of spelling notwithstanding) for Waterman S. Bodey, who found gold close by on July 20, 1859. Bodey died four months later in a blinding snow storm. You can visit his grave in the cemetery above the town. The community witnessed the extraction of some $100 million in gold and gained a reputation for murders, robberies and gambling, until approximately 95 percent of the town burned down in 1932. Still there's plenty of interest to see, and a state park brochure will guide you. For a place so remote, the visitor count is surprisingly high. It's running now around 150,000 a year. If you decide to fuel the statistic, expect to pay an entrance fee, and observe the park hours of 9:00 a.m. to 6:00 p.m. You'll want two to four hours here.

Twenty miles and forty minutes should bring you to the Mono County seat community of **Bridgeport.** Consider stopping for lunch and a look at the 1880 courthouse; but five hundred population does not a city make.

Further Explorations

If you are staying over an extra day, one thing you might consider is a hike to and through the fissures of Black Point, immediately north of Mono Lake.

Also, it's well to be aware of the Mono Lake Foundation Workshops offered annually from June to October. These are similar in concept to those offered by the Yosemite Association (see Chapter 26). Simply to give you a general idea of the types of workshops offered, let me quote the list for August of 1992:

Wildflowers of the Mono Basin
Fall Bird Migration of the Eastern Sierra
Glaciers Past and Present
Mono Basin Family Nature Exploration
Mono-Bodie Historical Tour
Writing and the Natural World

All these are weekend experiences, and all are offered at a discount to persons who are Mono Lake Committee members.

You say you don't have a whole weekend? All right; here's an activity that lasts about an hour: the **Natural History Canoe Tour.** It's offered Saturdays and Sundays, from mid-June to mid-September, at 8:00, 9:30 and 11:00 a.m. Place: South Tufa Reserve. Reservations strongly recommended. Call 619/647-6595. (Sorry, no children under 4 years of age.)

Best Time to Go

The window of opportunity is largely defined by the Sierra snow pack. Usually you can cross the passes by Memorial Day, and generally you can keep on crossing through October.

Early and late hold attractive pluses; early for lots of water in streams and falls; and late for glorious fall color, especially the vibrant yellows of the quaking aspen.

Nuts 'n' Bolts

This trip is long. The roads are well marked, but the driving may be slow.

Key Contacts

June Lake Chamber of Commerce
June Lake, CA 93529
619/648-7584

Lee Vining Chamber of Commerce
P. O. Box 130
Lee Vining, CA 93541
619/647-6629

The Mono Lake Committee
P. O. Box 29
Lee Vining, CA 93541
619/647-6595

U.S. Forest Service
P. O. Box 10
Lee Vining, CA 93541
619/647-6525

Bodie State Historic Park
P. O. Box 515
Bridgeport, CA 93517
916/525-7232 (District Office)

CHAPTER **40**

Ancient Bristlecone
Pine Forest

If you'd like to walk among the oldest trees in the world, this trip is definitely for you, even though, admittedly, it is a long reach from the San Joaquin Valley. It entails, in fact, more driving than any other trip in the book, but it's absolutely worth it! Supposing you must take this trip on a weekend, here's one feasible scenario: drive to Lee Vining or Bishop on Friday after work. Both towns offer motels and area campgrounds, such as Oh! Ridge just east of June Lake. You might even consider a second overnight in Bishop or Lee Vining, using Sunday to get home. Don't hurry. There's much to enjoy along the way.

On Saturday, head south from Bishop on Highway 395. After 15.5 miles (at Big Pine), turn left on Highway 168. Constantly climbing through sagebrush, pinon pines and Utah juniper, proceed 13 miles to a well-marked left turn. Now on a well-surfaced road cruise right on up to the Schulman Grove (10.5 miles).

Do you know what trees rank as the world's oldest? The answer, of course, is Bristlecone pines (*Pinus longaeva*). That comes as a surprise to quite a few people who were previously taught that either the Coastal Redwoods (*Sequoia sempervirens*) or the Sierra Big Trees (*Sequoiadendron giganteum*) were the earth's most ancient trees, with a probable age of 2,000 years. Then, not long after World War II, the word came down: "Hold on!" said the scientific community, "We were wrong. The oldest trees are the Bristlecone pines, some of which are over 4,000 years old!"

191

Using a device called a Swedish Increment Borer, scientists extracted pencil-shaped sections of trunk from some Bristlecone pines. These they put under a microscope and carefully counted the tightly compacted rings, each ring representing one year. In 1957 Dr. Edmund Schulman of the Laboratory of Tree Ring Research at the University of Arizona reported finding a tree that germinated in 2724 BC—making it 4,718 years old in 1994. Ponder that a moment. Here's a tree that was approaching 1500 years of age when Moses led the Israelites out of Egypt somewhere around 1230 BC.

In a scientific discipline called dendroclimatology, people can look at the spaces between tree rings and say: That was a terrible year weather-wise; it has to be the year that such and such a volcano erupted and substantially reduced the sun's impact on planet earth for months on end. Then, with the year of the eruption accurately pegged, events correlated with it can be dated with new exactness. So Bristlecone pines can give the world a weather history spanning four and a half millenia.

Where you can easily move among these living monuments is, roughly speaking, out back of Bishop. It's a 20,000-acre reserve which was set aside in 1958 as a Botanical Area to be administered for scientific study and public enjoyment. It lies within the White Mountain District of Inyo National Forest and so is under U.S. Forest Service management.

Let me tell you a bit about my own visit. I went initially to the Schulman Memorial Grove Visitor Center at 10,100-feet, where the pavement ends. There I learned by listening and by walking. First, I heard a talk by the resident naturalist, who sparked my interest in these trees by telling me the facts I've just shared with you. The climatic conditions in this district are so hostile that the trees have an average annual growing season of a scant six weeks. It takes them three years to produce a mature cone. The wood is very hard, containing a resin that serves as a fine preservative, so the trees are virtually immune to decay. Very gradually, exposed surfaces may be slightly reduced by the impact of sand and ice particles borne by winds of up to 200 m.p.h. The trees have neither the height nor the girth of the redwoods, but they have the strength necessary for survival in such a hostile environment.

The second thing I did was to hike the Discovery Trail with a good on-site trail guide in hand. Physically, what you face here is ½ mile of uphill, replete with switchbacks, followed by ½ mile of downhill. Along the way I met Pine Alpha, the first Bristlecone to be definitely determined to be more than 4,000 years old. It holds no records for height or girth, but at a glance you can tell it's been through a lot. Much of it is dead, yet it clings to life.

In my eagerness to do it all, I drove an additional 13.2 miles to the Patriarch Grove. I counted the grove itself a distinct pleasure. It contains the world's largest Bristlecone, "The Patriarch," with a circumference of 36 feet, 8 inches. It also features very young trees and trees of middle age. The ⅓-mile nature trail was easy despite its 11,200-feet elevation. I really liked being there, but I hated getting there. The 13.2 miles seemed to me interminable; and would you believe this? It was 13.2 miles back! I paid about 50 minutes twice for the pleasure of 45 minutes at the grove. I don't advise it. If you have time and stamina, you might be better advised to hike the Methuselah Walk. It's a 4¼-mile hike that begins near the Visitor Center.

It may interest you to know that on the upper slopes of 14,246-foot White Mountain the University of California maintains a pair of unusual scientific outposts: the White Mountain High Altitude Research Stations. In operation since 1950, the stations give scientists a base for studying the effects of high elevation on man, plants and animals. If you think of year-round residency, the personnel here live higher than anyone else in the continental U.S. They and their supplies are generally ferried in and out by helicopter on a run which is the highest in the nation.

Suppose there were no Bristlecones and no scientific research. Would I still recommend the trip? Absolutely! Because of the world-class vistas. For instance, when you're stopped at 9,280-foot Sierra Viewpoint, before you the sheer eastern side of the Sierra soars above the Owens Valley. Jagged peaks surpassing 14,000 feet stab the deep blue sky, leaving in one's memory lasting images of John Muir's beloved "range of light." I'm eager to go again.

Further Explorations

Driving the June Lake Loop, visiting the South Tufa Reserve at Mono Lake, and stopping at the U.S. Forest Service's Mono Basin Scenic Area Visitor Center just north of Lee Vining are three things which could be easily grafted onto this trip. For descriptions of these options, see Chapter 39. If you have additional time, you could profitably spend several days investigating a plethora of venues in and around the city of Mammoth Lakes (population 4,500; elevation 7,500 feet). Here's a short list: Mammoth Lakes Basin; a gondola ride to the top of Mammoth Mountain (elevation 11,053 feet); Hot Creek State Fish Hatchery and Hot Creek Geologic Site (boiling springs); Inyo Craters; and by shuttle bus plus some hiking, Devil's Postpile National Monument, Rainbow Falls, and Sotcher Lake. For further information, call the Mammoth Lakes Visitors Bureau at 800/367-6572.

Best Time to Go

This is an easy one: when the naturalist is on duty, ordinarily from about June 15th to Sept. 15th.

Nuts 'n' Bolts

The distance from Lee Vining to Merced is 144 miles, and I would budget a little over three hours for driving time .

Special note: Heed this official advisory. There are no commercial facilities after leaving Big Pine. Be sure you have a well-filled gas tank, drinking water and a picnic lunch. The USFS asked me to stress that *there is absolutely no drinking water up top. It's extremely important that you bring water with you.*

Key Contact

Eastern Sierra Interpretive Association
White Mountain Ranger Station
798 N. Main St.
Bishop, CA 93514
619/873-2500

Photo: Stephen McMillan

About the Author

Bill Sanford is a native Californian who has lived the better part of his life in California's Central Valley. He was educated at the University of the Pacific in Stockton; the Pacific School of Religion in Berkeley; and at St. Andrews University in Scotland on a Rotary Foundation Fellowship, after which he served as a United Methodist minister in half a dozen central California communities and abroad.

Although his work and travels have taken him to some 20 countries, he always loves coming home. Currently, you might find him writing another travel article, practicing the baritone horn, snapping photos, or following his love of railroads, when he is not working with Habitat for Humanity of Merced County. But there's a good chance you will find him out hiking the hills and canyons of this diverse area he never tires of exploring.

Bill Sanford lives in Atwater, California, and is married to the former Jeanne Shelley of Pleasant Hill, a UC Berkeley graduate and public school teacher. They have three grown daughters: Susan of Petaluma, Laura of Walnut Creek and Cindy of Sacramento.